Good and Evil

12 Philosophers on How to Live

Edited by Andrew Irwin

Introduction by Rory Stewart

TLS

TLS Books
An imprint of HarperCollins*Publishers*
1 London Bridge Street
London SE1 9GF

The-TLS.co.uk

HarperCollins*Publishers*
Macken House, 39/40 Mayor Street Upper
Dublin 1, DO1 C9W8, Ireland

First published in Great Britain in 2025 by TLS Books

1

A catalogue record for this book is
available from the British Library

ISBN 978-0-00-874719-0

Typeset in Publico Text
Printed and bound in the UK using 100%
renewable electricity at CPI Group (UK) Ltd

MIX
Paper | Supporting
responsible forestry
FSC™ C007454
FSC
www.fsc.org

This book contains FSC™ certified paper and other controlled
sources to ensure responsible forest management.

For more information visit: www.harpercollins.co.uk/green

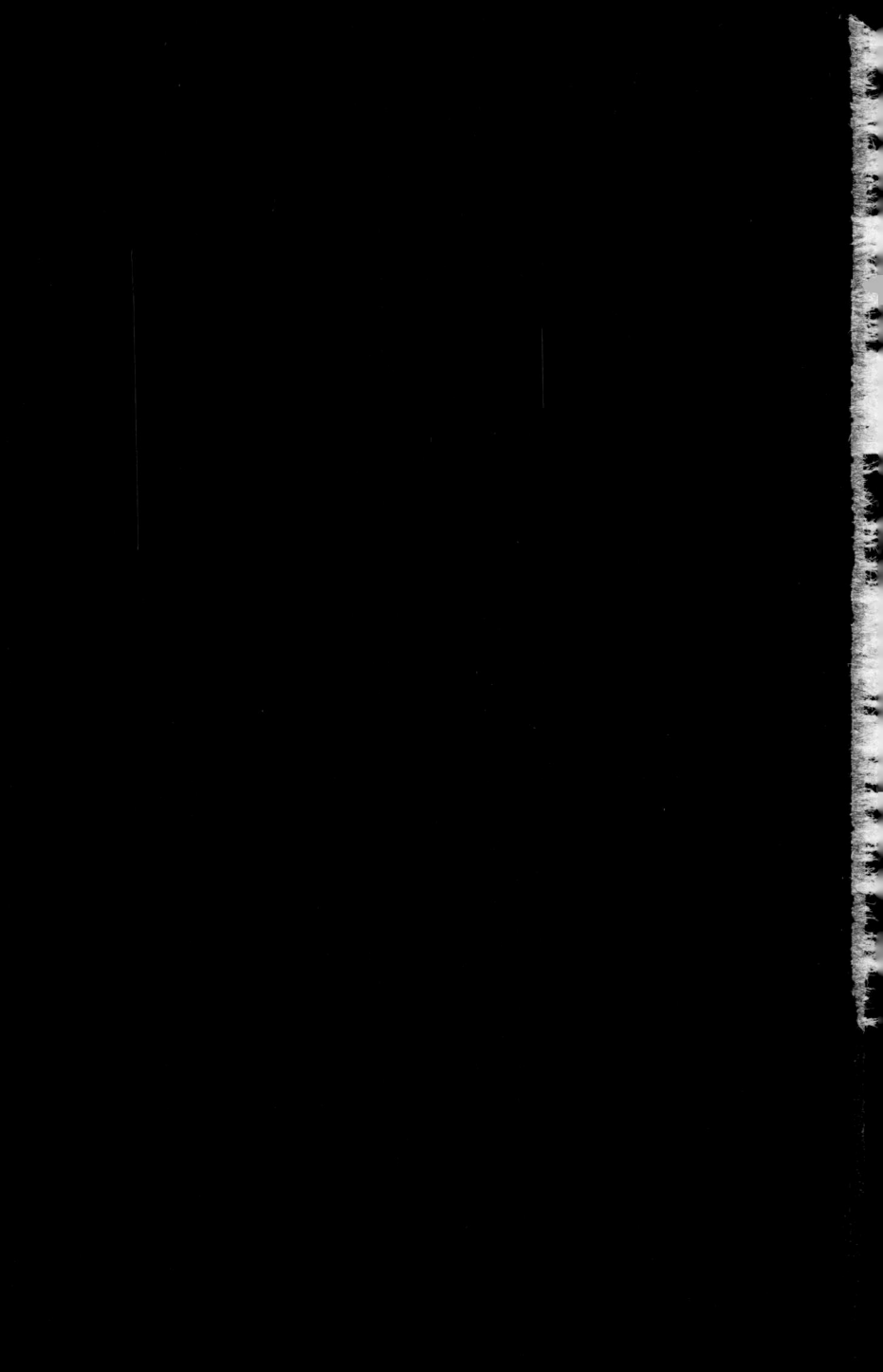

Good and Evil

Contents

Introduction

by Rory Stewart

A volume of short essays on great philosophers is a risky undertaking; a short introduction to such a collection, riskier still. Thinkers who produce theories of startling rigour and clarity can also be long-winded: John Stuart Mill's collected works span thirty-three volumes, Thomas Aquinas's *Summa Theologiae* alone runs to 1.8 million words; and these land masses of thought sit in vast oceans of commentary. JSTOR lists 100,000 scholarly articles surrounding Immanuel Kant; the University of Chicago counts 10,000 through which you might pass on your way to Niccolò Machiavelli.

The academics who contributed pieces to this collection can, and have, written such articles. But this is not their task in these essays, which are drawn from the *TLS*'s series, *Footnotes to Plato*. They have taken the risk of condensing philosophers and some of their central ideas to a few thousand words. Their academic colleagues will be conscious of the angles each writer takes in almost every sentence. And perhaps those colleagues will raise a scholarly eyebrow when more controversial assumptions are left implicit, or grumble at contested claims.

But there is an urgency, an edge and a richness to these essays, which could not be achieved in any other way. They are not in chronological order. Neither the philosophers, nor their biographers come from a single generation or school. The result, however, is far more than an assortment of shards and fragments. The unusual juxtapositions (jumping eight hundred years forwards from Aquinas to Hannah Arendt, and then two hundred backwards from Søren Kierkegaard to Gottfried Wilhelm Leibniz) reveal patterns and similarities in the philosophical landscape, and provoke unexpected dialogues of ideas.

Almost all these subjects were, we are reminded by these essays, brilliant as children. Mill had read all the major Latin writers by the age of nine and could read Plato and Demosthenes in Greek, easily, by ten. Leibniz at thirteen was composing 300 hexameters of Latin verse in a morning. Simone Weil and Simone de Beauvoir were in the same academic year, and came first and second, respectively, in their graduating cohort at the École Normale Supérieure. Friedrich Nietzsche was a professor at the age of twenty-four. But as necessary as their native intelligence was their refusal to subjugate their minds as they aged.

Viewed from a culture today which (at least in Silicon Valley) equates wealth with brains, these women and men were mostly materially 'unsuccessful' and in some cases startlingly poor. Not all of them shocked contemporaries as much as did Nietzsche, Kierkegaard and Beauvoir, but even the well-tempered Kant was censored and then banned from publication. Many rejected more comfortable careers – Aquinas refused the berth offered by his aristocratic family; Philippa Foot tried to surrender her lectureship to someone she believed more deserving; Weil took herself from a comfortable home to the brutalising factory floors and the front line of the Spanish Civil War. And they were not always 'well-adjusted'. Mill suffered a prolonged breakdown; Nietzsche died mad and Weil succumbed to starvation. These essays pay tribute not simply to their individual cleverness but to minds of terrifying rigour, focus, imagination and seriousness.

Each philosopher engages with aspects of the world which undermine, contradict or even refute traditional morality. Aquinas, Leibniz and Kant focus on the challenges which reason poses to morality, faith and God, and devote care and erudition to showing how logic, natural science and theology can still reinforce each other. Kierkegaard is a scandalising, isolated, brooding Danish thinker, producing furious paradoxes and tragic moral demands; Mill is an eminent Victorian humanist, economist, social reformer, member of parliament and utilitarian. This improbable pair (they were direct contemporaries) helped form many of our fundamental assumptions about the meaning of life, and the design of public policy today.

Machiavelli and Nietzsche represent the most radical opponents of such systems and consolations. Machiavelli attacks the virtue politics of Aristotle (a philosopher whom Aquinas – in the word of Angela Knobel's disarming anecdote – did so much 'to baptise'). Educated among Renaissance humanists who placed truth, generosity and mercy at the heart of leadership, Machiavelli not only argues that successful political leaders are dishonest, ungenerous and unmerciful, but seeks to demonstrate that they often should be (particularly, as William J. Connell explains, when founding a new state). The old idea that they must always be virtuous is, in Machiavelli's view, not simply naive but – because it undermines power – contemptible.

Nietzsche is more radical still. He mocks the foundations of Aquinas, Kant and Mill's ethics. Moral truths are cunning illusions, he argues – masks worn by power and resentment. The ideals of humility and equality are enervating and demeaning. God is dead, liberating man from the morality of Christianity, but leaving him with a vast absence to confront. Connell and Leiter's essays do not sugar-coat Machiavelli and Nietzsche. These thinkers'

4

views remain shocking and often profoundly depressing. This does not make them wrong. In fact, it is sometimes tempting to think that only complacency, conformism or cowardice prevents us from embracing their truths.

The most subtle and mesmerising responses to Machiavelli and Nietzsche's critiques can be found in the essays on four twentieth-century female philosophers – Hannah Arendt, Simone Weil, Philippa Foot and Iris Murdoch. (It is one of the strengths of this collection that Beauvoir – the exact contemporary and classmate of Weil – seems to occupy an entirely different intellectual space, her feminism beautifully expounded by Skye C. Cleary.)

Arendt and Weil were older, came from Jewish intellectual families in continental Europe, and were in their early twenties when Hitler took power. Both were deeply engaged with political movements and rejected stable academic careers; both were forced into exile, leaving friends and family who were later murdered in the Holocaust. The catastrophe, unfolding in their twenties, drew them away from the more abstract and formal traditions of philosophy, and towards contemporary history, political structures, psychology and capitalism. Essays by A. Rebecca Rozelle-Stone and Finn Bowring illuminate Weil and Arendt's developing sense that the evil of fascism was manifested, not through story-book villains but through 'normal' people whose carelessness, inattention and lack of imagination proved sufficient for mass murder to be enacted. (In Weil's words 'no desert is so dreary, monotonous and boring as evil'.)

Foot and Murdoch, almost fifteen years their junior, come from the more insular and settled context of Anglican England. Weil died because, even when diagnosed with tuberculosis, she refused to eat more than the tiny amount she believed people to be eating in occupied Europe. If her life resembles that of a medieval martyr, Foot's, in Rachael Wiseman's account, is that of an Oxford don with a patient and generous fifty-year commitment to the work of the charity Oxfam. Foot and Murdoch, however, were also strongly affected by the war – in part because they arrived at Oxford to find a university depleted of men (many of the male professors had been called up, and most of the male undergraduates were enlisted only a year or two into their degrees).

All four women emerge in this collection as suspicious of abstraction and reduction, and painfully aware of the limits of applying rigid universal rules. They share a sense that one of the central problems of moral life lies in living alongside other human beings. For Weil the requirement is for attention: that is, for suppressing all the mind's temptations towards fantasy and distraction, and forcing it to focus on reality – which can often feel inert, tedious or unpleasant. For Foot, the emphasis is on the patient, slow development of the art of moral understanding. For Arendt, the essence of 'plurality' lies in different perspectives which together develop meaning, affection and attentiveness. Each woman was wary of the excess and extremes of modern life. All saw morality as depending on careful contextual thought. All focused on the difficulty and disappointments, profundity, intricacy and joy of moral relations.

As these essays demonstrate, all four women also succeeded in giving new power and relevance to moral ideals, which had seemed to Nietzsche and many dominant twentieth-century philosophers to be exhausted, anachronistic and indefensible. Equality, dignity and human rights mattered once more when whole categories of fellow humans had been exterminated. Arendt and Weil both emphasised how fascism and the modern world were marked by a flight from truth and the demands of a difficult reality. The horrors produced by propaganda gave new importance to the careful explication of truth. After Hitler, thinking seemed more morally significant, morality more real. In Anil Gomes's phrase on Murdoch 'the lessons of the war seemed to be that there is such a thing as getting it right or wrong, and that it mattered that one get it right'.

Such conclusions, baldly stated, can seem disconcertingly simple, but when traced back to the original texts, we find not sonorous platitudes but intricately wrought arguments tested against the hardest facts. These women return us to the rawer edges of reality, facing the totalitarian horrors of the twentieth century, and they respond not with despair but with imagination and, ultimately, hope. Weil was insistently a Christian and her moral philosophy based in Jesus. Even the least explicitly religious of her concepts – 'attention' – drew on mystical traditions, rooted in meditation and the awareness of the mind's illusions. But even the moral realism of the other three, developed independently of any doctrine of God, was reinforced with metaphors and concepts whose genealogy lay in religion. Arendt was an atheist. But when, in Bowring's words, she argues that action reveals our unique capacity 'to break free of causal relations, by bringing something into being that is new and improbable', she reaches for a religious metaphor. 'Action', Arendt writes, is 'the one miracle-working faculty of mankind.' Foot's ethics restore exactly the private virtues of humility and compassion that Nietzsche had tried to mock in Christianity. For Murdoch, the key to all moral action is love.

All twelve of these essays work as intellectual cleavers cutting through the marrow of our lives. They exemplify Arendt's vision of thinking as a task which, like Penelope's shroud, must be continually undone so as to be remade each day. They demonstrate that the struggle against ignorance and dogma demands not simply perpetual effort, but often brutal self-abnegation and self-criticism.

Through the compressed lenses of these essays, these contemporary writers and their historical subjects vindicate philosophy's importance to the most intimate aspects of our lives, and its capacity to provoke, shatter and sustain.

Thomas Aquinas

by Angela Knobel

Years ago, when I was a graduate student at the University of Notre Dame, I had a desk on the seventh floor of the Theodore Hesburgh Library. Every so often, I would run into the library's elderly namesake in the elevator. The genial Father Hesburgh, always wanting to be friendly and never remembering that we had met before, would invariably ask what I was studying. 'Oh, Thomas Aquinas!' he would exclaim. 'You know, Aquinas baptised Aristotle.' And then the elevator would arrive at my floor and we would go our separate ways.

People often say, as a kind of quick and comprehensible summary of what he achieved and why he matters, that Aquinas 'baptised' Aristotle. The appropriation and transformation of Aristotle's philosophy (which certainly might be called a baptism) is one of Aquinas's central achievements. But too much of a focus on what Aquinas did for Aristotle can minimise the former's contributions to metaphysics, epistemology, systematic theology, the philosophy of religion and, of course, ethics. Underpinning them all was a vision of the intellectual enterprise itself: a belief in the fundamental unity of faith and reason.

Thomas Aquinas was born in about 1225, probably at his family's castle, Roccasecca, in the Neapolitan county of Aquino (the 'Aquinas' in Thomas Aquinas is not a last name, but a description of where he is from). Like many other youngest sons of noble birth, Thomas was destined for the priesthood. His parents sent him at a young age to study at the nearby Benedictine abbey of Montecasino, where his uncle was abbot, and where it was hoped young Thomas would one day become abbot himself. After several years at Montecasino, the teenage Thomas was sent to study the liberal arts in Naples. In Naples, Aquinas encountered two things that marked his life forever: the works of Aristotle (newly available in Latin) and a new order of priests, devoted to preaching and sworn to poverty: the Dominicans.

Aquinas wanted, and tried, to leave the Benedictines for the Dominicans, but his family had other ideas. His older brothers tracked him down and forcibly returned him to Roccasecca. Despite his family's attempts at dissuasion (which involved, among other things, imprisonment in Roccasecca for a year), Aquinas remained determined to join the Dominicans. When his family relented, Aquinas returned to Naples, and then moved on to the new University of Paris. There he received his bachelor's degree and became a professor himself, first as master of theology and later as master of philosophy. Over the course of his relatively short career (he is thought to have died around the age of forty-eight) Aquinas produced a staggering amount of scholarly work, around 8 million words: his *Summa Theologiae* (a comprehensive explanation of theology), the *Summa Contra Gentiles* (a defence of the rationality of Christian belief), extensive commentaries on scripture, commentaries on Peter Lombard's *Sentences*, sermons, *Disputed Questions* on various topics and a variety of other works.

Today few things seem less inflammatory than the study of the great ancient Greek philosopher Aristotle. The thirteenth-century University of Paris, however, was a site of political and theological controversy, and a great deal of that controversy had to do with 'the Philosopher' (as Aquinas called him). Latin translations of his work were first made available in medieval Europe in the late twelfth and early thirteenth centuries by Arabic commentators. Aristotle offered a scientific approach to philosophy that many in the medieval world found compelling, but he was also a pagan and affirmed many claims that Christianity denied. He held, for instance, that the world was eternal (rather than created by God) and that the human soul perished along with the body (a thesis that made an afterlife impossible). The University of Paris more than once banned the teaching of his works. By the time of Aquinas's arrival at the university, Aristotle's works were widely taught but remained controversial, and for good reason – for at the heart of the controversy was the relationship between faith and reason itself. What should one do when reason seemingly points towards conclusions that contradict one's faith? Should one ignore reason? Ignore faith? Embrace both and ignore the difference?

Aquinas's great insight was to see that faith and reason do not, and should not, conflict with one another. He held that if our reason is given to us by a good God, and if God gives us the gift of reason so that we might know and love him, then it should be impossible for the right use of that gift to lead us away from God. In other words, Aquinas saw that faith and reason do not seek separate truths. To the contrary, there is *one* truth, approached in different ways. Faith, Aquinas held, may well reveal truths that human reason could not arrive at on its own and cannot even fully comprehend. But (he argued) even with respect to truths that exceed our comprehension, there cannot be an outright contradiction between faith and reason. The truths we arrive at through the (correct) use of our reason can never culminate in the *denial* of God's revealed truths. The believer's approach to the deliverances of human reason, either their own or the compelling rational arguments made by thinkers like Aristotle, should be one of confidence, not fear. If faith and reason sometimes seem to point in opposite directions, Aquinas believed, then it is a sign that an interpretative and intellectual mistake has been made.

Aquinas's confidence in the ultimate harmony between faith and reason gave him the freedom not only to embrace but also to transform Aristotle's philosophy. These transformations were many; I'll limit myself to one foundational example.

One of Aristotle's weightiest achievements was his philosophy of nature, sometimes called 'naturalism'. Naturalism has many forms, but at the most basic level it is a philosophical theory that holds that the things one finds in the world, from plants to animals to human beings, are set apart from one another by their distinct 'natures', which not only cause them to be what they are, but also point them towards their fulfilment. A tadpole, for instance, is in some sense already a frog, even though it does not (yet) jump or sit on lily pads or catch insects on its tongue: it does not do these things, but if all goes well it *will* do those things, because it is already in the process of becoming a frog. For Aristotle, this is because from its very inception the tadpole has the *nature* of a frog, and its froggy nature both determines what its adult form will be and gives it impetus towards realising that potential.

The idea of a 'nature' is helpful philosophically. Plato, who taught Aristotle at his Academy, had already introduced the notion of 'forms' – eternal unchanging ideas that things in the world participate in, and which cause them to be what they are. For instance, we encounter various triangular objects in the world, and we can draw triangles ourselves. But no object that we encounter or create can ever perfectly exemplify triangularity. And yet we are able to recognise even very imperfect representatives of them as triangles. Why? Plato held that this is because we have encountered the eternal 'form' of the triangle, and are thus able to recognise imperfect participations in that idea. But Plato held that forms are separate from the things that participate in them. Aristotle's notion of nature allowed him to locate form *within* things themselves, providing a natural thing with its definition and purpose while at the same time being inextricably tied up with the thing itself.

However philosophically useful they are, Aristotle's ideas can appear to be at odds with Christianity, especially where human nature is concerned. Because for Aristotle they are internal to a thing and tied up with its 'matter', 'natures' seem philosophically incompatible with the idea that a soul can persist after the death of the body. More problematic still, an Aristotelian ethic implies that human beings are the primary agents of their own perfection, a thesis Christianity has consistently rejected.

Finally, since Aristotle had no account of how natures come to be, a naturalistic philosophy conflicts with the idea of a creator God.

Aquinas insisted that one could embrace both Aristotelian naturalism and Christian belief. With characteristic humility, he even argued that the seeds of that compatibility are inherent in Aristotle's own account. The Aristotelian account of nature intended to offer both a 'what' and a 'why': it can seem that in explaining *what* frogs are, Aristotle takes himself to have offered an account of *why* frogs are. Aquinas, though, saw – and thought Aristotle saw, too – that nothing in the notion of a nature explains *why* things are: a thing's nature cannot account for its existence. I can advance very far in my knowledge of frogs, but none of that knowledge can explain the existence of frogs. In everything we encounter in the natural world, Aquinas argued, what it is, its 'essence', is distinct from its existence. Since essence cannot account for existence, existence must be explained by something else. That explanation, Aquinas argued, must be found in the source of all things, God. Only in that source are existence and essence the same.

If Aristotelian naturalism could accommodate the notion of a creator God, Aquinas believed it could also help to explain Christian understanding of the goal of human life. The Christian tradition in which Aquinas was formed held that one only finds true fulfilment in union with God, and that this union is made possible only through the freely given and utterly undeserved gift of divine grace, which – on this view – makes human beings participants in the divine life. But Aquinas saw that if grace perfects and elevates us, then there must also be something that is perfected and elevated by it, and he saw in the Aristotelian account of nature an excellent way of accounting for that something. Following the mighty North African theologian Augustine (and the Christian tradition that formed him), Aquinas held that God does not owe man salvation. God gives man a great gift merely by creating him, and a still further gift by making it possible for his creation to share in His life. Aquinas proposed that what God gives us in creation is a nature of the kind described by Aristotle, and that the further gift of grace perfects and transforms that nature. Adam and Eve's fall, Aquinas held, not only destroyed the gift of grace but also damaged even the substratum (nature) that grace perfects.

Distinctions like these allowed Aquinas to propose answers to questions about the ethical life that had plagued Christian writers for centuries. Christians have always held, for instance, that all true goodness comes from God: it is through God's grace, not human effort, that one becomes capable of acting morally and of attaining true fulfilment. Even while affirming that view, though, Christians acknowledged the existence of apparent counter-examples. The Roman emperor Trajan, for instance, was certainly no Christian. Yet as emperor he instituted programmes to help widows, built orphanages and hospitals and even expressed reluctance to punish upstart Christians for practising their beliefs. Trajan and many other pagans seemed not only as good as, but even morally superior to, many believing Christians. Aquinas's incorporation of the Aristotelian notion of nature enabled him to recognise and embrace the idea that there could be true moral goodness in unbelievers like Trajan while nonetheless still insisting on the possibility of a more perfect, infinitely higher, kind of moral goodness.

Aquinas held that any rational being has the capacity to recognise and pursue what reason requires. He held that as one tries to bring one's acts into conformity with reason, usually with the help of teachers, one makes progress towards the fulfilment of one's rational human nature. And Aquinas agreed that many pagans could make such progress and, in doing so, achieve a real form of moral goodness. He simply held that there was a higher kind of goodness – the goodness of nature transformed and perfected by divine grace. In cultivating Aristotelian moral goodness, one becomes disposed to such grace. Aquinas thus held onto the idea that true fulfilment requires the divine, while accommodating what common sense tells us: that there are outstanding examples of moral goodness to be found everywhere.

These examples offer a glimpse of what it means to welcome truth wherever one finds it. Aquinas lived in a culture that saw Aristotle as a threat to its deepest principles. Yet Aquinas did not find Aristotle threatening. He retained his certainty in the truth and a willingness to welcome it, even when it appeared in unexpected places. A great deal has changed in eight hundred years, but a great deal remains the same: we still feel threatened by views different from our own, and inclined to react by rejecting them in their entirety. Aquinas shows us a different path: we can look for what is true, confident that what we find can only help us more fully to understand whatever portion of the truth we already possess.

Angela Knobel is an Associate Professor of Philosophy at the University of Dallas. Her books include Aquinas and the Infused Moral Virtues, *2021.*

Hannah Arendt

by Finn Bowring

Amid the concern that we live in a 'post-truth' world of radically incompatible knowledge claims, it is easy to lose sight of that other mental faculty, the faculty of thinking. Whereas knowing is a 'world-building activity', Hannah Arendt (1906–1975) wrote in *The Life of the Mind* (1978), and should thus contribute to the treasures of civilisation, thinking, like Penelope with her shroud, 'undoes every morning what it had finished the night before'. Thinking is the source not of truth but of meaning. It flirts with doubt, perplexity and wonder, and because of this it is the enemy not just of ideological dogmatism but of all forms of intellectual complacency and elitism.

Born in Hanover in 1906, and raised by secular Jewish parents in the Prussian city of Königsberg, Arendt studied Greek and Latin as a teenager, and devoured the work of Immanuel Kant, Søren Kierkegaard and

Karl Jaspers. She attended Martin Heidegger's ground-breaking seminars on Greek philosophy at Marburg University, and had a clandestine love affair with him during the 1920s.

Fleeing Nazi Germany in 1933, Arendt worked in Paris as a writer and activist helping Jewish refugees. In 1941 she managed to escape occupied France and board a boat to New York. There she became director of research for the Commission on European Jewish Cultural Reconstruction, an organisation tasked with recovering heirless Jewish property, including book collections and unpublished manuscripts. She left this role to work as an editor for Schocken Books, and then supplemented her salary, once she had gained American citizenship in 1950, by forging an itinerant but illustrious career lecturing in political thought at a variety of prestigious American universities. She saw herself as a political scientist rather than a philosopher. She advocated a kind of revolutionary liberalism, founded on a 'romantic sympathy' for the council system, a territorially organised non-party model of direct democracy, in which citizen assemblies elected their own delegates to represent them at each successive level of (local, regional, state, national) government. She wanted to reclaim the eighteenth-century idea of 'happiness' as a public good realised through political participation – a participation that might include acts of civil disobedience.

Since the 1930s Arendt had supported the project to establish a Jewish homeland in Palestine, favouring a political system of mixed Arab–Jewish municipal councils. But she opposed the idea of a Jewish state, seeing in Zionist nationalism an ugly repetition of the racist chauvinism from which the European Jews had fled. Her study of Bolshevism and Nazism, *The Origins of Totalitarianism* (1951), and her commentary on the trial of Adolf Eichmann, *Eichmann in Jerusalem* (1963), are Arendt's best known and most explicit discussions of the European catastrophe of the 1930s and 40s. Sandwiched between these texts was *The Human Condition* (1958). The title she gave the German edition of the book – *Vita Activa* – indicated that she saw this text as addressing the 'active' dimension of human existence. Her study of the *vita contemplativa* began much later, and was still incomplete when she died of a heart attack in 1975.

Arendt's initial focus on human activity was in part a reaction against the prejudices of intellectualism, which she believed had haunted western philosophy since its inception, and which seemed to have permitted countless educated Germans to accept, if not support, the creeping horrors of Nazism. In *The Origins of Totalitarianism* Arendt argued that Nazism and Stalinism constituted a radical break with the political history of the Occident. But she also believed that the very tradition of western thought was ill equipped to recognise and resist the currents of racism and fascism that began to surface in the last decade of the nineteenth century. Its fateful error had been to elevate thinking over doing, and thus to treat the often messy world of politics as a disposable adjunct to the flawless realm of ideas – to a doctrine or ideology.

In *The Human Condition*, Arendt divided human activity into a tripartite hierarchy. The lowest activity is the laborious task of transforming the organic environment into human sustenance – what Marx referred to as the 'eternal natural necessity which mediates the metabolism between man and nature'. Arendt called labour a 'worldless' activity, because it contributes nothing beyond the perpetuation of an ultimately perishable life, and because it testifies to that aspect of human existence that is shared by all organic things. The lowly status of labour in Greek antiquity is reflected in the way survival activities were hidden from sight in the household (*oikos*), and performed by the lowest-ranked inhabitants of the Greek city state (women and slaves). Labour often required strength, if not physical violence, which was exercised both over recalcitrant nature and, by the ruler of the household, over those who laboured. But never was the necessary domination of people or nature confused with freedom, the function of slavery being to liberate citizens from the burden of labour so that they could take their public place among a community of equals: 'if it were true that nothing is sweeter than to give commands and to rule others', Arendt pointed out, 'the master would never have left his household.'

Part of the superiority of 'work' over labour, Arendt argued, is that it redeems human beings from worldlessness. Work is a higher activity because to work is to fabricate a stable and lasting world of objects capable of protecting humans from the forces of nature. The highest accomplishments of *homo faber* are works of art, which transcend the criteria of need and usefulness and whose beauty may shine through the centuries. But the worker remains an instrumentalist at heart, and this leads to another problem, which is the haemorrhaging of meaning from a world where everything can be reduced to a practical purpose. For Arendt, activity has meaning only when it is done 'for the sake of' values and ideals; the worker, however, acts 'in order to' bring about a practical end, and that end, once achieved, can be used for the accomplishment of other ends.

For Arendt, the highest activity available to human beings is the public deed – to which she simply gave the term 'action'. As the Greek city-states, and later ancient Rome, expanded and became more politically organised, the substance of human action shifted from the daring deeds of the fabled Homeric hero to the more ordinary faculty of speech, and in this process 'freedom' became the political act of participation in public dialogue.

Action, Arendt argued, remedies the meaninglessness of human life by revealing our unique capacity to say and do the unforeseen, to break free of causal relations and means – ends reasoning by bringing something into being that is new and improbable. Action, she famously wrote, is 'the one miracle-working faculty of man'.

The freedom and novelty of action transcend the utilitarianism of *homo faber*, but action also gives meaning to human life by bringing into existence a common world which leads us out of ourselves, relating and separating us at the same time. Arendt called this the condition of 'plurality'. We share the world with other unique people, and the claim it makes on our affection and attentiveness grows when we exchange different perspectives on it. For us to believe in a common, three-dimensional world more solid and more lasting than our partial and fleeting selves, we need to see that world from a plurality of standpoints: 'the more peoples there are in the world who stand in some particular relationship with one another, the more world there is to form between them, and the larger and richer that world will be'. This, one might say, is Arendt's epistemological cubism.

Arendt's hierarchical model of human activities informed her critique of modernity. The conception of political action as the highest expression of humanness has always stood in tension with the idea that politics, like labour, is a necessary and regrettable means. From

Plato to Heidegger, philosophers have often regarded the practical business of politics as a soulless instrument, made necessary by humans' biological dependence on one another, for organising social life so as to permit the higher end of solitary thinking. For modern citizens, similarly, political participation is commonly regarded as a vehicle for asserting one's self-interest, which in most cases means protecting or increasing one's level of private consumption. (Self-interest, Arendt frequently argued, is a misnomer, since *inter est* refers to the common world that lies *between* individuals, not inside them.)

For professional politicians, politics is the means for the management of economic growth. As capitalism developed, what was left of the 'public sphere' was swallowed up by the market, and organic metaphors redolent of *animal laborans* – growth and abundance, the natural cycles of trade, earning a living – came to dominate political discourse. The economy – which for the Greeks was the laborious realm of necessity that had to be dealt with in order to facilitate the higher activities of public life – instead came to be seen as a living organism, and feeding it the job of politicians and public servants. A similar picture appears in the world of work, where few have knowledge and control of the things they create, and where organisational processes and procedures swallow up the ingenuity of the maker.

For all that is said about the 'materialism' of the afflu-ent society, Arendt pointed out that consumer capitalism is a system founded on relentless destruction, planned obsolescence and the manufacturing of urgent needs at ever higher levels of abundance (what Ivan Illich called the 'modernisation of poverty'). We treat consumer goods like the perishable products of our never-ending metabolism with nature, Arendt observed in *The Human Condition*. We turn homes into tradeable financial assets, and the most functional of goods are swept up into the frenzy of transient fashions. Instead of cherishing a stable world of things, the objects that last longest in this world are the things we care least about – they are the ever-expanding landfill sites that house the constantly discarded products of our throw-away society.

The paradox of capitalism's apparent success, then, is that instead of conquering necessity and delivering humans from want, the system of production has become a means for 'the channelling of nature's never-ending processes into the human world'. The economic world now functions like a kind of second nature – an 'unnatu-ral nature', and a 'pseudo world', as Arendt puts it. In the totalitarian regimes of Stalin and Hitler, this subordi-nation of human beings to natural, or quasi-natural, processes, was taken to its absolute extreme. Human worldliness requires the construction of a shared world of stable objects, tools, laws and institutions, which intercede between people and the relentless processes of nature and thereby create the space for political association and the steady negotiation and pursuit of common goals. Characteristic of totalitarianism, however, is the assimilation of process and movement into the very fabric of social and political life.

Arendt explicitly repudiated a causal explanation of totalitarianism, noting how 'the road to totalitarian domination leads through many intermediate stages for which we can find numerous analogies and precedents'. She said that imperialism, antisemitism, racism, mass unemployment, statelessness and the crisis of the nation-state system following the First World War were distinctive phenomena that had crystallised to produce a catastrophe few could have foreseen. Precursors to Nazism and Stalinism, however, were the late nineteenth-century movements of pan-Germanism and pan-Slavism, which explicitly called themselves 'movements' in order to signal their distrust of political parties and national parliaments.

The pan-movements were based on a mood of restless excitement and constant motion rather than a formalised political programme. The totalitarian movements that succeeded them exploited the lonely and rootless masses who had no stake in a corrupt and disintegrating political system, offering them – as an alternative to a harsh, confusing and often hypocritical reality – an ideologically consistent but fictional world whose inner coherence defied all factual evidence. They then set about creating an environment of violence aimed at degrading people to the status of fearful and unthinking animals, violence that became so arbitrary and extreme that all appeals to reason and common sense lost their validity. Above all, totalitarianism used movement, process and change as a terrorising force superior to any legal rule made by humans. For the cynical, the disaffected and the disenfranchised, totalitarianism offered a seductive sense of purpose and belonging. But this meant belonging to an irresistible movement of History or Nature in the face of which all human beings were essentially superfluous.

In her later study of Eichmann, Arendt revised her assessment of the role of ideology. 'Eichmann was much less influenced by ideology than I assumed in the book on totalitarianism', she wrote in a letter to her friend, the novelist Mary McCarthy. 'The impact of ideology upon the individual may have been overrated by me.' Her famous account of evil's 'banality' was an attempt to make sense of what she described as Eichmann's 'extraordinary shallowness', which 'was not stupidity but a curious, quite authentic inability to think'. Sent by the *New Yorker* magazine to cover the trial in Jerusalem, Arendt was shocked to discover that Eichmann was not the monstrously ideological antisemite that the prosecutors had described. Rather than implementing the Holocaust with 'fanatical zeal' and 'unquenchable blood thirst', as the judgement of the Court of Appeal put it, the criminal Arendt encountered was a diligent bureaucrat and cliché-loving careerist, a mass murderer who, in Arendt's words, 'probably did not even have the guts to kill'. Incapable of accounting for himself in anything but mindless platitudes, his last words before his execution were those of a stock funeral oratory. Arendt described how at his execution, Eichmann drank half a bottle of wine and then appeared impatient to mount the scaffold. This was followed by a speech which was so jovial and silly it sounded like he was a drunk visitor at someone else's funeral. He began by saying that he didn't believe in life after death, before declaring: 'After a short while, gentlemen, *we shall all meet again* … Long live Germany, long live Argentina, long live Austria. *I shall not forget them*'. Already incapable of thinking, looking and seeing, it was no surprise that he refused the offer of a blindfold at the moment of his death.

Arendt's insistence that dreadful things could be done by unexceptional people inevitably led her to consider the role in the Holocaust played both by ordinary Germans and, more controversially, by the Councils of Jewish Elders – the *Judenräte* that the Nazis set up to help manage the transportation of Jews to the death camps. Her careless description of the 'role of the Jewish leaders in the destruction of their own people' as 'undoubtedly the darkest chapter of the whole dark story' understandably angered many Jews, including some erstwhile friends. Gershom Scholem objected on the grounds that no one could judge who wasn't there; Arendt pointed out that the same argument was made by lawyers defending the Nazi war criminals. 'The problem, the personal problem, was not what our enemies did but what our friends did', Arendt said in an interview shortly afterwards. Whether she also had her one-time mentor Heidegger in mind here, given his notorious support for the Nazi party, is unclear.

What was Arendt really demanding from her friends? What obstacles can our culture raise against people's functional complicity with evil? When she finally turned, in the 1970s, to the second part of the human condition – the life of the mind – she returned again to Socrates, and to the way Socrates cultivated not just a dialogue with his fellow citizens, but an inner conversation with himself. In thinking, Arendt argued, one develops 'the disposition to live together explicitly with oneself', and this functions as a brake on the temptation to do wrong: 'It is better to suffer wrong than to do wrong, because you can remain the friend of the sufferer; who would want to live together with a murderer?'

Arendt recognised that thinking is not a political activity, but that it should at least prevent us from participating in the violation of human fellowship. As the public exchange of opinions recedes before the social-media universe of self-confirming facts, thinking may offer a sanctuary for the sceptical mind and an inward rehearsal of the outer conversation that constitutes a political community.

Finn Bowring is the author of Hannah Arendt: A Critical Introduction, *2011, and a senior lecturer at Cardiff University. His latest book is* Trouble with Death: Making Sense of Mortality in the Anthropocene, *2025.*

Simone de Beauvoir

by Skye C. Cleary

Soon after Simone de Beauvoir's *Le Deuxième Sexe* (1949) was published in France to great acclaim, Blanche Knopf, co-founder of the publishing house Alfred A. Knopf, Inc., in New York, heard about it. Excited by the buzz, and initially under the impression that it was a sex manual, she sought the advice of an expert in sexual behaviour: a retired zoology professor and insect specialist named Howard M. Parshley. He told her that the book was not dogmatically feminist, but 'intelligent, learned, and well-balanced', and was subsequently asked to translate it into English.

Beauvoir (1908–1986) wrote *The Second Sex* after female suffrage had already taken hold (in 1944), and her philosophy unintentionally inspired a new 'wave' of feminism that eventually ushered in no-fault divorce, academic gender studies, greater access to education, and contraception; and which made sexual discrimination at work and marital rape illegal, and granted women other rights that helped them to overcome being what Beauvoir called 'prey to the species' and to take control of their own destiny. Beauvoir wrote *The Second Sex* as a theoretical work; yet she was pleased that it inspired activists, such as Betty Friedan, Gloria Steinem and Kate Millett. In an interview with Jean-Louis Servan-Schreiber for French television in 1975, Beauvoir said that at first she had thought overthrowing capitalism would resolve the inequalities between the sexes. It was only later that she realised the situation of women was no better in the USSR, Czechoslovakia or the Communist Party than it was in capitalist societies, and she decided to become more actively engaged in the feminist struggle.

Beauvoir conceived of existentialism as a living and practical philosophy. She did plenty of theorising, too – but her goal was to think through concrete problems, exploring potential solutions. She published essays, as well as novels, plays, memoirs and personal letters, which gave her more freedom to explore the challenges of the human condition.

For example, Jean-Pierre – a character in Beauvoir's play *Les Bouches Inutiles* (1945; *Who Shall Die?*, 1983) – is disgusted with the way his town in fourteenth-century Flanders is being managed; he turns down a prestigious government job in the name of keeping his hands clean. But when he finds out that the administration plans to banish women, children, the old and the weak from the town during a siege, he regrets his quietism. 'What stupid arrogance!' he tells the woman he loves. 'I was a coward, and I have condemned you to die by remaining silent.' He campaigns for the government to change its policy so as to respect the basic human rights of its citizens – and succeeds. Jean-Pierre's realisation reflects Beauvoir's broad call to action: to become *engagé* – to be active participants in creating the conditions of our lives.

Beauvoir was reluctant to be categorised as an existentialist, or even philosopher, but posterity begs to differ. She has since become one of the most widely read philosophers, existentialist thinkers and feminists of all time – largely because of *The Second Sex*, although in 1954, her novel *Les Mandarins* also won the Prix Goncourt.

Beauvoir began *The Second Sex* with the question: 'What is a woman?' The answer was complex. What started as an essay evolved into almost 1,000 pages of historical and philosophical analysis, which took her just fourteen months to write. As Beauvoir developed her philosophy in Parisian cafés in the 1940s, she became acutely aware of the inequalities between the sexes. Underpinning the book is the Sartrean maxim that 'existence precedes essence', meaning that we are thrown into the world (we exist) and then create our being (our essence) through our choices. If we're prevented from choosing, that's oppression; if we choose to give up our freedom, that's what Beauvoir called a 'moral fault'. *The Second Sex* became an in-depth philosophical investigation of how oppression, and women's acceptance of it, shaped their situations.

The emphasis on situation is one of the key factors that distinguishes Beauvoir from other existentialists. For Beauvoir, we are free, but we are also thrown into contexts in which we don't always have the freedom to choose. This is very different from Jean-Paul Sartre's emphasis on radical freedom; by his lights, any attempt to blame our situation for our predicament is a denial of freedom – a form of bad faith. In *L'Être et le néant* (1943; *Being and Nothingness*, 1956) Sartre imagined an impassable crag, and suggested that it's only impassable if one has imagined that it would be possible to climb it. In her attack on this idea, Beauvoir argues in *The Ethics of Ambiguity* (1947) that, 'If a door refuses to open, let us accept not opening it and there we are free. But by doing that, one manages only to save an abstract notion of freedom. It is emptied of all content and all truth'. Whereas for Sartre, 'success is not important to freedom', Beauvoir's point is that without the *possibility* of action – if situations enchain us – then freedom is rendered impotent. We may be free to scale a crag, but unless we have the power to do so, such freedom means nothing.

Beauvoir's most revolutionary idea, which appeared in *The Second Sex*, is that, 'One is not born, but rather becomes, woman'. The meaning of this has been debated ever since. One way it can be understood is that although sex is biological, gender is socially, culturally constructed. The biological facts of a woman's body do not mean necessarily that her role in society is to be a mother and housewife or that a man's role is to be the breadwinner. Beauvoir argued that flawed logic such as this – overemphasising the biological aspects of life and reducing people to their anatomy – had been used to keep women in their role as 'the second sex'.

We are all rooted in biology, but that doesn't limit our futures in any meaningful way – hence Beauvoir's statement that 'within the human collectivity nothing is natural'. We can't deny the facts of our bodies – what she calls our 'facticity' – but the assumption that our biology sets a specific destiny for us is mere prejudice. Gestating babies is a natural female animal function; the obligation to rear children is not. Rather it's an engagement, a commitment that is chosen or rejected. Differences in the ways the sexes assert themselves are more about our situation than some 'mysterious essence'. Although Beauvoir comes dangerously close to victim-blaming when she says that women have been complicit in their oppression because they put up with it, she also acknowledges that women's 'acceptance' was often a problem-solving strategy to negotiate the traditions, roles and constraints imposed on them.

This is where Beauvoir's nuanced point about situation reaches its climax. Yes, we're free, but it is always freedom *in situation*. Our freedom is violated when we're in situations that close down the possibility of choosing an open future. Those who are stuck in ignorance or oppressive situations are robbed of their freedom. Individuals can rebel against it, yet challenging social norms often comes at a high cost, which is why *The Second Sex* concludes with an urgent call to action for collective change – for women to challenge their oppression, embrace their freedom and live authentically by pursuing self-chosen projects and careers. The first step is economic independence; but we also need moral, social and cultural changes for relationships between the sexes to become ones of fraternity, friendship and love instead of conquests and defeats. In an interview with Susan J. Brison in 1976, Beauvoir said, 'I'm certain, in fact, that this idea of domination is one of the features of the masculine universe that must be totally destroyed, that we must look for reciprocity, collaboration, etc'.

Beauvoir's ideas about how situations modify freedom also have a wider application, beyond feminism, to discussions on punishment, forgiveness and vengeance. Originally published in 1946 in *Les temps modernes* – a French journal edited by Sartre, Beauvoir, Maurice Merleau-Ponty, Raymond Aron and others – Beauvoir's essay 'An Eye for an Eye', written amid the war trials in the aftermath of the Second World War, considers the situation of criminals and the desire for vengeance.

Justice, Beauvoir proposes, affirms that we have a reciprocal relationship with other people, and if this relationship is disrupted, we want them to 'pay for it', to restore an equivalence to our situation. Imagine you're in a crowded place and you're pushed. It feels like you're a mere obstacle for the other, an object, a thing. You want an acknowledgement that the reciprocity between you and the pusher has been violated. An apology can quickly disarm the situation and restore the respect between you and the other. If an apology is not forthcoming, it's not unusual to want justice. Perhaps you address the perpetrator in a more-or-less polite manner, perhaps you look daggers at them, or give them a shove in return. This desire for restitution doesn't just hold on a personal level – it's an effort to maintain a level of respect between all of us. Beauvoir writes that 'the respect that he demands for himself, each person claims for his loved ones and finally for all men'.

Though one may well be angry at being pushed, usually the shover isn't evil. More likely, it was an accident, or perhaps carelessness. Evil people *will* terrible things on others. For Beauvoir, 'an abomination arises only at the moment that a man treats fellow men like objects, when by torture, humiliation, servitude, assassination, one denies them their existence as men'. It's true that we're objects for others, but we're also subjects – and not to acknowledge this interior aspect of another's being is violent. For Sartre, we're always trying to reduce each other to an object, or reduce ourselves to an object for the other, and the attempt to rob one another of freedom forever traps us in sadomasochistic relationships. For Beauvoir, it's an atrocity and to deny another's subjectivity is the 'sole sin' against humanity.

Robert Brasillach, the Editor of the Fascist newspaper *Je suis partout*, committed Beauvoir's sole sin when, during the Nazi occupation of France, he published the pseudonyms and locations of French Jews, some of whom Beauvoir knew personally. Beauvoir sat in the press gallery during Brasillach's trial in a liberated Paris. When a petition circulated to save him from the death penalty, calling for 'solidarity as writers', Beauvoir refused to sign.

Punishment, Beauvoir thought, is a necessary evil against evil. If one is religious, one doesn't face this problem. God is the ultimate judge and 'He alone has the right to punish'. Others, however, face the problem of how to uphold human values. Beauvoir thought she understood Brasillach's situation reasonably well. She didn't want him dead. But, as she wrote in *Force of Circumstance, Volume One: After the war* (1963), 'there are words as murderous as gas chambers'. She didn't believe in a God who would deliver ultimate justice, and she couldn't excuse his advocacy of genocide.

Charles de Gaulle refused to pardon Brasillach, who was executed by firing squad. This might have seemed a proper punishment but, for Beauvoir, it was not true vengeance; the victimiser escaped the experience of being in a reciprocal situation. In 'An Eye for an Eye', Beauvoir notes, 'in dying he slips out of the world; he shrugs off his punishment'. Beauvoir thought it important to reinforce the notion that actions have consequences, that life and death have meaning, and that 'it is not shocking to affirm them at the cost of a life'.

However, just as it's absurd to hate a natural disaster for killing people, so too it is absurd to hate common criminals who do not intentionally violate our humanity. Soldiers in war, Beauvoir suggests, don't deserve to be hated – not only because they act under orders, but because on both sides, the soldiers are in reciprocal situations.

Common crimes might seem horrendous in an objective sense. Yet, Beauvoir proposes, it's a different story when we take into account the subjective experience of the perpetrator. Maybe the perpetrator made a mistake, or succumbed to an unfortunate impulse. Maybe they thought they were doing what was in their best interests at the time, or maybe they just weren't thinking at all. We shouldn't be so quick to judge. Again, in 'An Eye for an Eye', she writes:

It requires a lot of arrogance and very little imagination to judge another. How can one measure the temptations a man could have faced? How can one appreciate the weight of the circumstances that give an act its real shape? One would have to bring his upbringing, complexes, failures, and entire past – the totality of his engagement in the world – into account.

Brasillach published multiple names repeatedly, intentionally, and fully aware of the murderous consequences of his doing so. Yet, in cases where the crime is an aberration, Beauvoir recommends erring on the side of forgiveness, since not all victimisers degrade the other to a thing: they don't intentionally strip another person of subjectivity. A person might not understand what's wrong with their actions until they see them in a new light, through the eyes of their victims. In such cases, we should focus on rehabilitation instead of punishment. As Beauvoir writes:

One reeducates children, the ignorant, those populations that are ill-informed; one does not punish them. Neither does one punish the ill or those mad people in whom conscience has been annihilated. And everyone knows that even a normal adult always acts out of situations that he has not chosen, that numerous physiological and sociological factors weigh on him.

To understand is to accept, and if we understand the situation, the subjective experience of the victimiser, then often the crimes lose much of what makes them awful. In one of her more controversial statements, Beauvoir goes so far as to say, 'One could explain even Hitler's conduct, if one knew him well enough'. Still, for Beauvoir, explaining a situation doesn't mean forgiving it. Even in those cases when we do understand the situation, all we understand is the context in which a person chooses. 'Certainly, man is wretched, scattered, mired in the given, but he is also a free being. He can reject the most urgent temptations.'

Beauvoir's acknowledgement of the tension between freedom and facticity reveals itself here again: it's true that we're free and responsible for our actions, but we're also clogged in situations. For Beauvoir, as for Sartre, we are the sum of our actions, but we're also more than that. We're also our future and intentions. We can't escape our past actions, but we ought not to be slaves to them – and we ought not to reduce people to being slaves to their past – because people can always redeem themselves through new actions. As she writes:

Can one condemn an entire man on the basis of
one moment of his life? This would be all the
more cruel because this weakness that one
reproaches him for is already in the past. It does
not exist anymore as the expression of a
freedom, but as something fixed that the guilty
party trails behind him in spite of himself. Since
he is other than the person who committed the
crime, can we still hate him? And what good is
served by punishment?

Ultimately, Beauvoir argues that 'all punishment is
partially a failure' because, to restore justice in the world,
to make someone really pay for their crime, they need to
experience the horror of it. That means not only the
suffering, but also the situation of the victim. When those
in concentration camps were freed, and slaughtered
their jailers, they came close to successful vengeance
because, she says, 'the victims and their torturers had
really exchanged situations'.

Nevertheless, Beauvoir is reluctant to allow for private
vengeance. Certainly, 'an eye for an eye, a tooth for a
tooth' has what she calls 'a whiff of magic. It strives to
satisfy some unknown dark god of symmetry. And, above
all, it corresponds to a profound human need'. But the
principle serves only to send avengers floundering into a
bottomless quagmire of revenge and injustice.

Social justice might be enticing, but without due process it risks descending into a tyranny: those seeking vengeance can get carried away with their will to power; they make mistakes, and the wrong people are punished. Court trials aim to address such issues, but Beauvoir points out that they too are flawed. Often they're an exercise in drama and pomp, where disinterested judges following abstract processes dish out arbitrary punishments that are so far removed from the crime they don't provide any reasonable restitution for the wrong committed. While we might be tempted to think that objectivity in the courtroom is ideal, Beauvoir, in 'An Eye for an Eye', counters:

> The official tribunals claim to take refuge behind an objectivity ... They want to be only an expression of impersonal right and deliver verdicts that would be nothing more than the subsumption of a particular case under a universal law. But the accused exists in his singularity, and his concrete presence does not take on the guise of an abstract symbol so easily.

This is, however, the system we have. And a problem with Beauvoir's approach is that there is no concrete way to understand whether a victimiser intentionally treats another as an object, or whether there is some other motivation. The purpose of courts is to take such things into account, but whether they do so in an effective manner is another question.

The implication of Beauvoir's thinking, nonetheless, is that there are better paths than vengeance: education, rehabilitation and putting our confidence in people to redeem themselves. Forgiving doesn't mean forgetting or letting people get away with atrocities; rather, it means being attuned to individuals' situations, respecting one another and upholding the dignity of humankind. Whether it's the tension between the sexes or between victim and victimiser, reciprocity and collaboration provide a clearer path towards fraternity and friendship. We're all 'gnawed away by nothingness', as Beauvoir says; we are all adrift in the world together and find ourselves in ambiguous situations as our freedoms bump into one another; but our lives are also interconnected and mutually supporting, like the stones in an arch. Such is the human condition, Beauvoir writes: 'For we have not only to establish what our situation is, we have to choose it in the very heart of its ambiguity'.

Skye C. Cleary teaches at Columbia University and is the author of How to Be You: Simone de Beauvoir and the Art of Authentic Living, *2022.*

Philippa Foot

by Rachael Wiseman

Philippa Foot (née Bosanquet; 1920–2010) was brought up in a large country house in Yorkshire, and educated at home by a series of governesses. Her childhood was blighted by illness and loneliness. As an adult she wondered what her mother had been thinking, letting her go out riding alone at the age of nine. A question that remained with her to her final years was that of happiness. What makes a life a happy one? To what extent is a person's happiness an objective matter? Can a life filled with trial and pain be happy if it is lived with courage, friendship and generosity?

When her final governess, who had been to university, told her young charge that such a thing was possible for her too, Philippa seized on it as a chance to escape. She took extra coaching and a correspondence course and crammed just enough Latin to get through the Oxford entrance exam. Foot chose Somerville College because she'd heard that Lady Margaret Hall was 'socially OK and that Somerville wasn't'. 'Somerville then for me', she resolved. Her mother was opposed, but Foot proved herself an exceptional student, gaining a first in Philosophy, Politics and Economics even though she spent much of her final year bedridden with a recurrence of childhood tuberculosis. Despite her brilliance, her early lack of education left her doubting herself. She spent her undergraduate years in fear of being 'sent away from Somerville for incompetence in philosophy'. In later years she would often put herself down: 'I'm not terribly clever; quite intuitive but not very clever'.

Foot arrived at Oxford in 1939 in the final months of the so-called 'Phoney War'. With many of the male dons away doing war work, undergraduates received an unusual education. She learned about Immanuel Kant with the refugee scholar Heinz Cassirer and took tutorials with the conscientious objector and theologian Donald MacKinnon. 'No one has influenced me more', she later said of MacKinnon. 'He created me.' Among those her own age, Foot quickly befriended Ruth Collingwood (daughter of the Idealist philosopher R. G. Collingwood). In the year ahead of her at Somerville, and studying Classics, were Mary Midgley and Iris Murdoch. Though Foot initially thought Midgley intellectually intimidating and Murdoch a troublemaker, the trio soon became close. After graduating, Foot and Murdoch moved to

London, where they lived together in a single-room attic flat for the remainder of the war.

Foot was determined to be a moral philosopher in 1945 following the publication of pictures of the newly liberated Bergen-Belsen concentration camp. 'The news was shattering in a way that no one now can easily understand. We had thought that something like this could not happen', she recalled. Though her main interest at the time was philosophy of mind, she saw a pressing need for work in ethics that could make sense of this new reality. The non-cognitivist moral philosophy that dominated at Oxford was not, she thought, suited to the task. While 'cognitivist' theories focus on the role of knowledge, understanding and judgement (cognition), non-cognitivist theories highlight the role of emotion, desire and impulse. According to non-cognitivism the question of what a person ought to do (morally speaking) depends on his or her subjective desires, projects, or personal principles, and not on objective moral facts. A. J. Ayer, C. L. Stevenson and R. M. Hare were contemporaries of Foot's who argued for well-known versions of this approach, which has historical roots in the eighteenth-century empiricist David Hume. According to such a philosophy, a sincere moral judgement ('Murder is wrong', say) necessarily goes beyond 'description' or 'assertion of fact' to include a subjective evaluative component which depends on the preferences and feelings of the individual making the judgement. It follows that for someone with a suitably unusual set of motivations and principles, the Nazis' actions would be (for him) morally right. Someone who wanted to convince such a person to stop being a Nazi could not appeal to objective facts about what is good or bad, virtuous or vicious. For Hare, moral argument was restricted to seeking internal inconsistencies in one's opponent's principles, showing that their desires and projects would be better served by other means, or bringing to their attention morally neutral facts that might be relevant to their deliberations. For Foot this was not enough. She wanted to be able to say to a Nazi that whatever his principles, feelings and commitments, he was wrong, and that his being wrong was a matter of fact.

In a trio of influential early papers ('When is a Principle a Moral Principle?', 'Moral Beliefs' and 'Moral Arguments'), Foot took aim at the non-cognitivists' view of moral judgement. Her opponents, she argued, had a problem when it comes to saying what counts as a *moral* principle or belief. Most people have a pretty clear intuitive sense of which principles are the moral ones. 'Don't be cruel' is; 'Don't look at hedgehogs by the light of the moon' isn't. (This example is Foot's.) But because non-cognitivists tie morality to individual preference, Foot points out, they have no way to get their distinction to line up with our ordinary one. For them, the difference between a moral and non-moral principle is merely formal: a principle is a moral principle if and only if a person holds that it applies universally. That is, if one holds not just that one oughtn't to be cruel *now*, but that *no one* ought to be cruel *ever*. But because this is a merely formal condition, it follows that the hedgehog principle, if adopted by someone suitably fanatical, would count as part of his morality. Against this, Foot argues that the term 'moral' indicates that the matter at hand is connected, in some way, to objective facts about benefit and harm, and to what is of serious importance in human life. 'Don't be cruel' clearly counts by this standard, but it is difficult to imagine how the hedgehog principle could have this standing. That said, Foot points out that seemingly non-moral beliefs may turn out to be moral if viewed against a wider background. 'Don't wear buttons' appears non-moral, but if viewed in the context of a religious outlook that abhors pride and ostentation and sees simple and plain dress as an outward display of humility, it may come to be seen as a serious matter and so count as part of a morality.

In 'Moral Arguments', Foot urges a view of moral disagreement where resolution requires a complex negotiation over the application of 'specialist moral concepts', like 'pride', 'ostentation', 'rude', 'cruel', 'just', and 'kind'. Foot argues that these terms, which connect with concepts like character, virtue, harm and benefit, are descriptive. The reason we often disagree about their application is not that they are less factual than non-evaluative descriptions, but rather that their application depends on the complex background pattern of human life. Here her thought resonates with that of Iris Murdoch: morality is as much a matter of how one sees things as how one acts.

Crucial to Foot's philosophical development at this time was her friendship with Elizabeth Anscombe. Anscombe was a research fellow at Oxford for much of the 1950s, during which time she worked with Ludwig Wittgenstein and then, after his death in 1951, edited his unpublished papers. Foot and Anscombe met most days in Somerville's senior common room, where they discussed Wittgenstein and (Anscombe's other great philosophical love) Thomas Aquinas. Hints of both are evident in those early papers. Foot describes her efforts to resist Anscombe, who used Foot as a willing test subject to try out Wittgenstein's arguments. 'Every week', wrote Foot, 'I was defeated and I thought of myself like a character in a child's comic where a steamroller has gone over them and you're just a silhouette on the ground – but you're there in the next episode.' In 1957, when Anscombe's fellowship was due to end, Foot offered to resign her lectureship in order to make a post available: 'I don't want to resign', she wrote to the college Principal, Dame Janet Vaughan, but 'if I am on to something in ethics I shall want her more than ever'.

As well as her work in moral theory, Foot published important papers in applied ethics, most notably on euthanasia and abortion. In both cases, as with her more abstract theorising, the line she takes involves careful attention to the realities of human life and sensitivity to the ways in which seemingly minute differences in context can profoundly affect the moral character of a situation. Such attention is precisely that which must be cultivated by a virtuous person – the exercise of virtue is not the formulaic application of universal rules ('Don't, ever, stare at hedgehogs!'), but the capacity to recognise what would count as courage, humility, justice or charity in a given situation. In her paper on euthanasia she considers when and whether an act of letting someone die (by withholding treatment, for example) or bringing about their death (by giving them poison) could be an act of charity or justice. She explores when an individual's desire to die matters to this question, and when it does not. Her conclusion is that while there are cases where even active euthanasia may be an exercise of justice and/ or charity, there is no easy argument connecting the justice of (some) individual acts of helping to die to the conclusion that such acts should be legalised. The dangers of abuse are numerous, and Foot warns that legalised active euthanasia 'might change the social scene in ways that would be very bad' and bring about a kind of 'spiritual disaster'.

Foot's paper on abortion is a study of the concept of justice, and the demands that it may make with regards to the life of others. She considers the Catholic doctrine that it is sometimes permissible to perform acts which one foresees will result in death, so long as the death is not something one aims at. For example: it may be permissible for a pilot to bomb an armament factory in order to destroy the enemy's manufacturing capacity, knowing it is likely that civilians will be killed, though it would be murder were he to bomb a civilian population in order to kill them. Foot argues that the question of 'side-effects' or 'unintended consequences' cannot do the argumentative work to which it has been put in cases where the act and consequence are intimately connected. Instead, she proposes, a distinction between negative duties (duties not to harm) and positive duties (duties to save) provides a better framework. She illustrates this distinction with the example of a runaway tram that is on course to hit five stranded workmen. The tram driver, in this now famous thought experiment, must decide whether to do nothing (and so let the tram kill the five), or act to save them by steering onto another track on which there is a single worker. Foot uses the example to explore the complex ways in which duties to save and duties not to harm interact in tragic situations.

Foot's work in the 1950s builds a case that moral judgements can have objective criteria – but there was one aspect of the non-cognitivist picture that she retained for many years. This was the idea that moral facts alone cannot give a person a reason to act: a shameless person may speak truly and truthfully when he says, 'I agree that, as a matter of objective fact, such-and-such is heartless, greedy and duplicitous; but that's not a reason for *me* not to do it'. What such a person lacks is the desire to do what morality recommends. For most of her life, Foot insisted that it would be perfectly rational (though scandalous) to lack such a desire, and so held that moral imperatives bind only to those who desire to be moral.

In a now infamous paper, 'Is morality a system of hypothetical imperatives?', Foot urges that there is no special, binding, 'moral ought' – that there is just the ordinary, hypothetical 'ought' that is always vulnerable to the rejoinder, 'But I don't want to!' She counsels that this should not dismay us. In many cases an argument in favour of cultivating a virtuous character can be made from considerations of self-interest – for example, there are long-term benefits to having an honest disposition and multifarious harms to having a reputation as a liar. And even when such arguments fail, as with the virtues of charity and justice that often require a person to act against his own interests (and *in extremis* to sacrifice his own life), Foot does not despair. She enjoins us to recognise the instinctual love of others that resides in the human heart (the fount of charity), and to see ourselves as 'volunteers in the army of duty' – a merry band of 'like-minded people fighting together against injustice and oppression'. Someone who does not wish to devote his life to this great cause is not, for Foot, irrational; but he thereby excludes himself from a project that is a great source of meaning, happiness and friendship.

Later in her life, Foot rejected this part of her philosophy, and came to argue that participation in the fight against justice was not voluntary, but was, after all, demanded by reason. Her argument against her former self is set out in her only monograph, the elegant *Natural Goodness*, published when she was eighty years old. She identifies as the problem in her former work an assumption about practical reason (reasoning about what to do) that is ubiquitous in philosophy, at least since David Hume. This is the idea that practical reason is reasoning about means and not ends. On this assumption, the criticism of someone's action as unreasonable can only amount to a criticism of his action as means to his chosen end. If I want to get rich it would be irrational for me to spend all my days lounging in bed, because lounging in bed is not likely to bring about that end. But on this view, my end – to get rich – cannot be criticised as practically irrational.

In *Natural Goodness*, Foot seeks to provide the resources to overthrow this assumption. She begins by establishing the idea of species-relative criteria of well-being. Statements about what is proper, normal, good, suitable or beneficial to living things of a certain kind are, she argues, both factual and normative. 'Squirrels bury nuts' both describes a form of behaviour that we can observe in squirrels, and introduces a normative standard against which the behaviour of an individual squirrel can be evaluated. There is, so to speak, something wrong if a squirrel does not do this, because nut-burying behaviour is one crucial way in which squirrels ensure they have enough food in the winter months.

Of course, no individual squirrel is 'perfect'. The descriptions of the squirrel's life-form do not combine to describe a perfect, Platonic squirrel, in relation to which all actual squirrels can be judged and found wanting. Rather, they give a squirrely pattern that particular squirrels live out in individual ways. A squirrel without a tail is defective, in the sense that it is a fact that squirrels have tails and that their tails help them to balance – something they need to avoid predators and get food. But a tailless squirrel, given a conducive environment and a bit of luck, might find novel ways to live out a perfectly good squirrely life. Nevertheless, questions like 'Is this squirrel flourishing?', 'Will this harm the squirrel or benefit him?' and 'What does this squirrel need?' relate an individual squirrel to its life-form. Such questions have answers that are both descriptive and normative. Thus, Foot introduces a framework in which to speak of 'natural goodness and badness for living things'.

With this framework in view, Foot argues that moral evaluations of goodness and badness in humans have the same relation to descriptions of the human form of life. Though practical rationality is, in many respects, that which distinguishes us from other living things, it can still be viewed as part of natural goodness for humans. The human capacity for practical reason is the capacity to choose well. Foot argues that if an individual is exercising her practical reason in a way that does not lead her to choose what is good for humans, there is something wrong with her (as there would be with a squirrel who did not bury nuts). Among those things that humans need in order to live well are the character traits named by virtue terms: these allow us to form the sorts of bonds of family, friendship and community that characterise our essentially social nature.

Thus, Foot concludes that the shameless person, described above, is straightforwardly mistaken. His practical reasoning is defective if he does not choose those things – kindness, charity, honesty – that are good for him. In this context, Foot asserts a broadly Aristotelian definition of happiness as the condition of flourishing, rather than as a subjective feeling. A hedonist who pursues pleasure over virtue is both unhappy and irrational, however much his life is one of sensory thrills.

Outside of philosophy, Philippa Foot is admired as an important figure in Oxfam's early history. She joined the 'Oxford Committee for Famine Relief' in 1942, just after its formation. In the early years she helped send donated clothes to refugees in occupied Europe, and later helped to run its first shop on Oxford's Broad Street. She appreciated its dashing and rebellious character, and the absence of social hierarchy among its board. When she was invited to give a lecture on 'Justice and Charity' for Oxfam's fiftieth anniversary, she prepared by knitting a blanket square – a reminder of the intricate relations between small acts of goodness and this now global charity.

Rachael Wiseman is Reader in Philosophy at the University of Liverpool. She is the co-author of Metaphysical Animals: How Four Women Brought Philosophy Back to Life, *2022.*

Immanuel Kant

by Allen W. Wood

Immanuel Kant (1724–1804) is the most influential of all modern philosophers. Virtually every philosophical movement since the end of the eighteenth century is some version, interpretation or variation on Kant's 'critical' philosophy, his 'transcendental turn', his 'Copernican revolution'. Kant's dominant influence is sometimes hard to understand and, especially for non-specialists, hard to accept. And much of his influence is due in part to various misunderstandings of his thought. Kant could write wittily and even elegantly when he wanted to. But he did not, like David Hume, think of himself as primarily 'a man of letters', and his aim was not, like René Descartes's, to publicise to the world in elegant prose a new conception of nature and science. His prose was couched in the forbidding jargon he inherited from the philosophical tradition of Christian Wolff in which he was educated.

I tell my students that they should be grateful for this, because that jargon is what connects Kant's often highly original ideas to the western philosophical tradition going back to the Greeks. Kant himself was not knowledgeable in that tradition. He came to philosophy from natural science – physics, astronomy, geology: what would then have been called 'natural philosophy'. Kant became a 'philosopher' in our sense of the word only when he began reflecting on the foundations of these emerging and changing departments of knowledge. It was not until relatively late in life that Kant's interests shifted to include ethics, politics and religion (though his final decade of philosophical activity was concentrated on them). The remarkable thing about Kant, to those who study him, is the striking originality and insight present in the dark corners of his seemingly obscure and forbidding prose.

Kant was a philosopher of the Enlightenment (*Aufklärung*). But what is 'enlightenment'? Many in Kant's time would have agreed with the definition put forward by one of Kant's greatest contemporaries, Moses Mendelssohn. For him, *enlightenment* was the education of our understanding or theoretical faculty aiming at knowledge, in contrast to *culture*, which is the education of our practical faculty aiming at virtue. But Kant offered a new twist that exposed the fundamental issue facing modern human beings. 'Enlightenment', he said, is 'the human being's release from self-incurred minority.' Minority is the condition of children, who do not govern or take responsibility for their own lives but must be guided by others. Minority is 'self-incurred' when it is due not (as with children) to the incapacity to direct one's own life, but instead to a lack of courage and resolution. This, Kant thinks, is the fundamental issue facing modern individuals. We must learn to think for ourselves rather than deferring to the authority of books, doctors, lawyers and clergy and letting them take the place of our understanding and our conscience.

It is all too easy to suppose Kant is recommending that we be idiosyncratic contrarians, contemptuous of tradition, authority and the thoughts of others. But that isn't so. By 'thinking' Kant means the use of understanding or reason subject to the basic standard of universal validity. To think for oneself, by Kant's lights, means to think from the standpoint of all others. Kant argues that the only way for individuals to become enlightened is to communicate freely with one another, so that each acquires the ability and confidence to think by using the thoughts of others as both an incitement and an (always fallible) external criterion for correct thinking. A culture of enlightenment is a *public* culture in which people learn to take responsibility for themselves by becoming cautiously confident of their capacities as they also become aware of their limitations.

In the title of Kant's most famous work, *Critique of Pure Reason* (1781), 'critique' comes from the Greek word for 'judge', and the title can be read in two senses – that is, the faculty of pure reason is both the judge and the object of judgement. We should strive to take both the measure of its (the faculty's) capacities, acquiring confidence in them, and the measure of its limits. Kant's *Critique* therefore has a double aim: to vindicate the possibility of empirical knowledge of nature (such as Newtonian physics), and to demonstrate the impossibility of theoretical knowledge about thinkable realities that cannot be perceived, such as God, the human soul and free will. Kant wants us to come to terms with what he calls our 'peculiar fate': we do, and should, raise questions about realities transcending the sensible world, but must resign ourselves to our incapacity to answer them. Kant's account of our cognitive faculties assumes that in order to cognise, we must both sense and think. The only objects of which we can have true cognition are sensible objects, material things in space and in time. But what makes this knowledge possible must come not from sensible data but from our own faculties and therefore must be *a priori*. To say that cognition is *a priori* is to say that we must ground it in the active exercise of our own faculties, not in the data presented to them. Kant rejects the idea of *innate* knowledge because he takes that to be something also presented to our faculties rather than created by them. *A priori* knowledge comes from both our sensibility and our understanding. We experience sensible objects only under spatio-temporal conditions, and these conditions afford us the *mathematical* foundations of modern physics. But our capacity to judge the objects that come before us in this way depends on the way our active faculties of understanding, imagination and judgement connect the data of the senses in lawlike ways, so that the physical world is made up of substances causally interacting according to necessary laws and giving us a unified reality we call 'nature'.

Kant's philosophy is said to have triggered a 'Copernican revolution'. Just as Copernicus changed our conception of the heavens by including the thought that we (as observers) are in motion rather than being the fixed centre of the universe, so Kant proposes to solve sceptical problems about causality, space and time by viewing the knowable world as relative to the activity of our faculties. Human knowledge is not the precise mirror of realities and relationships that exist entirely independently of us. Instead, the order of nature must be seen as an order that we, as knowers, create. Our own understanding, Kant says, is the true law-giver of nature.

One remarkable and baffling consequence of this Copernican revolution is Kant's claim that cognisable objects, while 'empirically real', are 'transcendentally ideal'. By considering the world not in common sense terms or those of science, but rather in light of the conditions of the possibility of knowing it, we must accept that we cognise only 'appearances' not 'things as they are in themselves'. Kant calls this doctrine 'transcendental idealism': some have taken this to be either a wild metaphysical doctrine deeply at odds with common sense, or else a radical scepticism that cuts us off entirely from true reality. Kant would reply that transcendental idealism expresses only the epistemic modesty or humility that goes with acknowledging our human limitations and taking responsibility for our active role in knowing.

However transcendental idealism is understood, Kant spends much of the *Critique* arguing that our reason generates ideas of objects that we can never cognise because they lie beyond the bounds of the senses. These include ideas involved in thinking of nature as a completed totality, and also supernatural ideas often found in religion; the ideas of God, free will and the immortal soul. Kant claims we can have no theoretical (scientific) knowledge of such objects; ideas of them can nonetheless play a role in our moral life and can also be represented indirectly (symbolically) in aesthetic and religious experiences that do not constitute a form of theoretical knowledge.

Kant's emphasis on our responsibility to, and for, ourselves individually, humanity's responsibility to itself collectively, and the role of humans in constituting the world underpin the Kantian conception of the *primacy of the practical*, and the centrality of ethics to his overall project. Moral philosophy rests on a fundamental principle or moral law, which is *a priori* in the sense that it comes from our reason as active beings rather than being a mere passive response to external influences, whether of our natural desires or the influence of others. But just as the fundamental standard of reason for Kant is universal validity for all rational beings, so the moral law is also conceived as a law for all rational beings conceived as an ideal community or *realm of ends*.

The basic value in Kant's ethics is that of human dignity – the rational nature in persons as an end in itself. A person is a being for whose sake we should act, and that has an unconditional claim on us. This is the source of what Kant calls a categorical imperative: a grounds for action that does not depend on any contingent desire of ours or aim to achieve any further goal. In the twentieth century, the American philosopher John Rawls corrected the basic and traditional misunderstanding of Kant's ethics when he said that it is not an ethics of stern command but rather one of self-esteem and mutual respect. To this I would add that Kant's ethics is also an ethics of caring or empathy – what the philosopher himself calls *Teilnehmung*: sympathetic participation. This is not sympathy merely in the sense of passive feeling for or with others, but instead an active taking part in the standpoint of the other which leads to understanding and concern.

Kantian ethics is rightly said to be an ethics of autonomy. But this is not to be taken in the sense that we fallible creatures legislate our own morality. Morality for Kant is objective and independent of anyone's will, even the divine will – which wills the good *because* it is good. Autonomy means instead that the authority of the moral law depends on our being able to regard it as legislated by our own will when we take the responsibility to conform ourselves to the moral law. In this way morality rests on the dignity of our rational nature, regarded as a value beyond price that must not be sacrificed to any other value.

Kant associates with the moral law a distinctive rational incentive, proper to morality and different from all contingent or empirical incentives. Readers are often put off by Kant's characterisation of this incentive as *duty*. But it is not a coercive incentive created by any will, divine or social, or any other that is external to us. Kant's most revealing name for the will that gives first place to the moral incentive is: *the good will*. Or better yet: *goodness of heart*. This is a caring for our own dignity and in relation to others a balance of love and respect. Kant holds that we tend to love that to which we feel superior, as parents tend to love their children more than the children love them. As Kant wryly puts it: 'Love, like water flows downward more easily than upward'. Respect is directed towards a worth in others that strikes down our self-conceit; it therefore infringes our self-esteem. Morality thus requires us to respect one another in order to prevent love from falling into contempt, and to love one another to prevent respect from falling into hatred. This requirement is called 'duty' because goodness of heart does not come easy to human beings. The kind of caring that comes easily and naturally demands little of us and flatters our self-esteem. True goodness of heart requires us to constrain ourselves to care in the right way.

Kant holds that we have duties *towards* ourselves and *towards* other rational beings. We have no duties *towards* beings unless they have rational wills of which we can be empirically aware. But we have duties towards ourselves *in regard to* beings such as God (whose rational will cannot be empirically known to us), and also to non-rational animals and the beauty and harmony of nature. Kantian ethics does not devalue non-rational nature, but views its value as imposing duties on us by way of our own respect for ourselves when we appreciate our limited place in nature and responsibility in relation to it.

Ethics for Kant is a system of duties, but also of virtues. Kantian ethics offers no decision procedure to tell us which actions we may or must perform. Kant's *Doctrine of Virtue* (1797) makes perfectly clear that his theory of duties does not tell us to decide what to do by formulating maxims and deciding by some procedure whether they are 'universalisable'. Though a popular image of Kant's ethics, it totally misunderstands its letter and its spirit. There is a common image of Kant's ethics as 'deontological' in the caricatured pejorative sense: a strict set of rules applying without exception. This rests on a basic mistake. Kantian ethics considers wrong all actions of certain kinds: lying, servility, envy, hatred, arrogance. But these kinds are designated by concepts in which moral judgements – required, forbidden, meritorious – are already included. It takes good judgement to know which acts fall under these morally laden concepts. All lies are necessarily wrong, but not all cases of false-speaking count as lies.

Kant distinguishes *ethics* or *virtue* – based on non-coercible obligations of rational self-constraint – from *right* or justice: the conditions of external freedom for all under universal law. For Kant, no human being may be rightfully coerced in the name of any end or any good, however lofty. Coercion may be justified only in the name of that very freedom that coercion would infringe. Freedom for all requires the coerced limitation of the freedom of everyone: my freedom must be limited by universal laws so that others may have the same freedom that I do. This is the basis of Kant's philosophy of law and the state. Moral incentives may be indispensable to the success of right or justice, but the standards of right do not rest on them.

Kant also made significant contributions to theories of aesthetics. His *Critique of the Power of Judgment* offered a truly revolutionary approach. Kant seeks a third way between *objective* theories that identify beauty with some objective property such as perfection – perhaps perfection apprehended sensibly rather than intellectually – and *subjective* theories that identify beauty with empirical pleasure, perhaps under certain idealised conditions involving disinterest or expertise. It roots the pure experience of beauty in the harmony between our faculty of sense or imagination and our faculty of understanding. We experience pleasure in beautiful objects as a result of the harmonious co-operation of these faculties; and that comes about when the object inspires greater harmony than is required for us to have mere objective cognition. What we consider beautiful is a perfection of form that pleases us through the way our faculties co-operate in our perception of it. The other basic aesthetic experience besides beauty is that of the sublime, which we experience in objects felt as so large as to be beyond our comprehension or so powerful as to overwhelm us entirely. The sublime is a combination of pleasure and displeasure, akin to the experience of respect. The sublime arises when we value an object but experience this value as the striking down of our self-conceit. For many in Kant's time, sublimity was associated with awe at the thought of the divine – fear of God. Kant acknowledges this as part of the insight of the monotheistic religions – Judaism, Christianity, Islam – which by withdrawing God from the senses made the emotional experience of God all the more powerful. But for Kant the sublime is really the experience of absolute value attaching to our moral vocation: its transcendence of nature and of everything we have achieved so far.

Kant's philosophy tells us to take responsibility for our own lives. It sees human understanding as the law-giver of nature, morality as resting on autonomy, aesthetic experience as dependent on our experience of our faculties and our moral vocation. We might think of it, therefore, as secular, anti-religious or irreligious, rejecting God's authority in a Promethean spirit. Kant would protest against this interpretation. For him, our moral vocation is ultimately to be part of an ethical community whose only model in human history has been religious and even ecclesiastical. He seeks not to reject religion but to understand it and reform it. Because our cognition is limited to the sensible world, we can relate to God only indirectly, through symbols that engage us practically and aesthetically. But the symbol must be distinguished from the reality it symbolises, and enlightenment requires us to take responsibility for interpreting religious symbols rather than submitting slavishly to their literal meaning. Kant himself viewed his philosophy as ultimately religious in import, even though it is also, and equally, a philosophy of critical reason and rational autonomy.

Kant is the philosopher of modernity, just as Aristotle is the philosopher of western antiquity. The values of enlightenment, critique, autonomy are what humanity still continues to live by – or at least strives to live by insofar as it lives up to its dignity. All philosophy since Kant belongs to that fundamentally Kantian striving.

Allen W. Wood is Ruth Norman Halls Professor at Indiana University and Ward W. and Priscilla B. Woods Professor emeritus at Stanford University.

Søren Kierkegaard

by Clare Carlisle

Søren Kierkegaard (1813–1855) thought, wrote and lived as both a philosopher and a spiritual seeker. His century saw the growth of modern universities, and an increasing professionalisation of intellectual labour. During the 1830s Kierkegaard was a theology student at the University of Copenhagen, where he received a broad education, discovering Romanticism and German Idealism as well as studying Christian theology and biblical exegesis. Yet he criticised academic philosophy as an abstract, overly rationalistic approach to the deep questions that arise from the human condition. In 1835 he wrote in his journal, 'I still accept an *imperative of knowledge* and that through it men may be influenced, but *then it must come alive in me*, and *this* is what I now recognize as the most important of all. This is what my soul thirsts for as the African deserts thirst for water ... This is what I needed to lead a *completely human life* and not merely one of *knowledge*'. Displaying the influence of Socrates on his intellectual formation, he added that 'a man must first learn to know himself before knowing anything else'. His first substantial work, completed in 1840, was his graduate dissertation, *On the Concept of Irony with Continual Reference to Socrates*, and Socrates remained Kierkegaard's chief philosophical inspiration until his death in Copenhagen's Royal Frederiks Hospital at the age of forty-two.

All philosophers ask questions, but Socrates' questions were peculiar, often designed to produce confusion rather than answers. While everyone else in ancient Athens was, as Kierkegaard put it, 'fully assured of their humanity, sure that they knew what it is to be a human being', Socrates devoted himself to the question *what does it mean to be human?* From this question flowed many others: *What is justice? What is courage? Where does our knowledge come from?* Cultured Athenians had ready answers to these questions, but Socrates' inquiries led in a new direction, away from what the world recognised as wisdom, and towards a higher truth. Kierkegaard also found a critique of worldly wisdom in Paul's First Letter to the Corinthians: 'I did not come with lofty words or human wisdom (*sophia*) as I proclaimed to you the mystery of God', Paul wrote to these Greeks: 'I came to you in weakness and much fear and trembling'. Paul urged the Christians in first-century Corinth – a city where, as in ancient Athens, many philosophers and rhetoricians peddled their pedagogic wares – to rest their faith 'not on human wisdom but on the power of God'.

Inspired by these subversive exemplars, Kierkegaard interrogated the assumptions of his own cultured contemporaries in nineteenth-century Denmark. They too appeared 'fully assured of their humanity', and Kierkegaard perceived that they were also, as citizens of a Lutheran nation and members of the Danish State Church, rather too secure in their Christian identity. In order to challenge the spiritual complacency of his age, Kierkegaard forged a new philosophical style. While other thinkers deduced propositions and built systems, he created satirical, elusive, undogmatic, lyrical, soul-searching, unsystematic works which eventually earned him a reputation as the 'father of existentialism'. These works influenced some of the most significant philosophers of the past century, including Martin Heidegger, Jean-Paul Sartre and Ludwig Wittgenstein. During Kierkegaard's lifetime, however, the feminist writer Fredrika Bremer aptly described him as a 'philosopher of the heart'. His extraordinary writing was rooted in the inward drama of being human, eschewing the more objective, systematic efforts to understand the natural world and global history that characterised nineteenth-century philosophy and science.

Kierkegaard's first book, *Either/Or* (1843), was – and probably still is – best known for its provocative 'Seducer's Diary'. This fictional work chronicles the pursuit of a young woman, Cordelia, through the streets and lanes of Copenhagen; the Seducer lures Cordelia into a weird psychological courtship, then ambiguously ends the affair, leaving her heartbroken. 'I am intoxicated by the thought that she is in my power ... now she is going to learn what a powerful force love is', this narrator declares gleefully. Readers were scandalised by his immorality, yet the book was a bestseller and critically acclaimed as well as denounced. Less notoriously, *Either/Or* ends with a rousing sermon that distils the spirit of Kierkegaardian philosophy:

> Perhaps my voice does not have enough power and intensity; perhaps it cannot penetrate into your innermost thought – Oh, but ask yourself, ask yourself with the solemn uncertainty with which you would turn to someone who you knew could determine your life's happiness with a single word, ask yourself even more earnestly – because in very truth it is a matter of salvation. Do not interrupt the flight of your soul; do not distress what is best in you; do not enfeeble your spirit with half wishes and half thoughts. Ask yourself and keep on asking until you find the

answer, for one may have known something many times, acknowledged it; one may have willed something many times, attempted it – and yet, only with the deep inner motion, only the heart's indescribable emotion, only that will convince you that what you have acknowledged belongs to you, that no power can take it from you – for only the truth that edifies you is true for you.

This idea of edification – meaning spiritual empowerment, inward deepening, 'strengthening in the inner being' – was central to Kierkegaard's authorship. He learned from Romantic authors to experiment with a variety of literary genres in order to edify his readers. At the same time, he saw it as his peculiar, Socratic task to make life, and especially spiritual life, more difficult for his fellow Christians. In *Concluding Unscientific Postscript* (1846) Kierkegaard described a philosopher in his early thirties – a figure much like himself – sitting in the Frederiksberg Gardens, smoking a cigar and meditating on his place in the world:

You are getting on, I said to myself, and becoming an old man without being anything ... Wherever you look about you on the other hand, in literature or in life, you see the names and figures

of the celebrities, the prized and acclaimed
making their appearances or being talked about,
the many benefactors of the age who know how
to make life more and more easy, some with
railways, others with omnibuses and steamships,
others with the telegraph, others through easily
grasped surveys and brief reports on everything
worth knowing.

This narrator reflects that spiritual life is also being made
easier by philosophical systems that elucidate the
Christian faith, and demonstrate its moral value to society. 'And what are you doing?' he asks himself –

Here my soliloquy was interrupted, for my cigar
was finished and a new one had to be lit. So I
smoked again, and then suddenly this thought
flashed through my mind: You must do
something, but since with your limited abilities it
will be impossible to make anything easier than it
has become, you must, with the same
humanitarian enthusiasm as the others, take it
upon yourself to make something more difficult.
This notion pleased me immensely, and at the
same time it flattered me to think that I would be
loved and esteemed for this effort by the whole
community.

Kierkegaard wrote these words not long after he had been cruelly caricatured in Copenhagen's satirical weekly *The Corsair*. For several weeks in 1846, Peter Klaestrup's cartoons mocked Kierkegaard's precious, imperious attitude to the reading public while exaggerating his thin legs and curved spine. Some images referenced his failed engagement to a young woman named Regine Olsen several years earlier, depicting him as at once exploitative and unmanly.

Even Kierkegaard's most devoted readers find that his commitment to deepening the difficulty of being human produced a slippery, often baffling series of writings, stubbornly resistant to summary and paraphrase, since so much is compressed between their lines. Within many of these texts, different narrative voices perform conflicts between life-views, with no clear resolution; they exhibit errors and misunderstandings as often as they proclaim truths. For Kierkegaard, the work of philosophy was not a swift trade in ready-to-wear ideas, but the production of deep spiritual effects that would penetrate his readers' hearts, and change them.

Indeed, his career as a philosopher was inseparable from his own change of heart: when he ended his engagement to Olsen in 1841, she was devastated and his reputation was in tatters. 'It was an insulting break, which not only aroused curiosity and gossip but also absolutely required that every decent person take the side of the injured party ... here at home harsh judge-ments were unanimously voiced against him. Disapproval, anger, and shame were as strong among those closest to him as anywhere', one of his nephews later recalled. The engagement was a fork in Kierkegaard's path through life. As he hinted in his philosophical novella *Repetition* (1843), breaking up with Regine made him an author. Instead of becoming a family man and a professional theologian or pastor in the Danish State Church – in short, an upstanding bourgeois citizen – he travelled to Berlin to pursue his philosophical studies, and began to write *Either/Or*.

This rambling, witty, sophisticated debut drew on Kierkegaard's personal experience to explore three different attitudes to life and love: the aesthetic, the ethi-cal and the religious. Put very simply, the aesthetic Seducer, who pursues his own pleasure, loves only himself; the ethical man, represented by a married Judge, loves another person, namely his wife; the reli-gious individual loves God, who is the ground of all his human relationships. Through these three characters Kierkegaard probed the philosophical and religious significance of marriage, the issue that had been the turning-point in his own life. At the same time, *Either/Or* was a polemical book. It undermined the fashionable Hegelian ideas of Kierkegaard's rival Hans Lassen Martensen, a successful professor of theology, and also subtly criticised the homely ethical Christianity taught by Bishop Mynster, the head of the Danish Church.

In the wake of Kierkegaard's broken engagement, *Either/Or* asked whether there can be a higher calling that justifies causing suffering to others and breaking with ethical norms. In other words, is there any claim on human beings that overrides the moral law? (Kant and Hegel had both offered interpretations of Christianity based on the principle that there is not, though they had different accounts of morality.) In *Fear and Trembling* (1843), Kierkegaard pursued this question further by means of an experimental 'dialectical lyric' on the biblical story of Abraham's journey to Mount Moriah to sacrifice his son Isaac. From this famous work – now a staple of the undergraduate philosophy curriculum – emerged an account of religious faith which emphasised its grave ethical stakes and high personal cost. Living in relation to God, argued Kierkegaard, risks 'the distress, the anxiety' of being misunderstood and shunned by other people. 'Knights of faith' like Abraham (and also Mary, the mother of Jesus) were not heroes in any worldly sense, though they came to be viewed as exemplars by later generations, once history had proved their transgressions – or sacrifices – worthwhile.

Yet Kierkegaard also criticised the other-worldly, ascetic, life-denying form of religion, represented most visibly in the renunciations of monks and hermits, which

Friedrich Nietzsche would excoriate a few decades later. *Fear and Trembling* depicts a 'knight of faith' who performs a miraculous 'double movement': he renounces the world and then returns to it, receiving it back as a gift from God. This movement echoes both Abraham's journey up and down Mount Moriah, and the Socratic philosopher's ascent from and return to the dark cave of ordinary social life. Kierkegaard's preferred spiritual archetype, however, is a ballet dancer, who leaps up away from the Earth (towards God) then descends just as gracefully, finding her balance in the world. 'To be able to fall down in such a way that the same moment it looks as if one were standing and walking, to transform the leap of life into a walk – that only the knight of faith can do', he wrote in *Fear and Trembling*.

Monasticism and marriage are two thematic poles in Kierkegaard's philosophy of religious life – two imaginative possibilities, neither of which he could live out himself. Denmark's monasteries had been dissolved following the Reformation. Though Kierkegaard's reasons for refusing to marry Regine remain ambiguous, it seems clear that the difficulty lay with marriage itself, rather than Regine, whom Kierkegaard continued to love, albeit in a rather idiosyncratic manner. As a historical figure, Kierkegaard is an interesting counterpoint to Martin Luther, who, unusually, was both a monk and a married man (though not at the same time). Indeed, one of the most significant consequences of Luther's Reformation was a shift from monasticism to marriage as the primary model of a Christian life, exemplified by Luther's own life choices. Kierkegaard obsessively explored both these life paths through his writing. Several of his works are attributed to pseudonyms who are monks or hermits, while his cast of characters includes faithful husbands who reflect on their marriages, and fiancés who break their engagements. While he also investigated traditional metaphysical topics, such as time, change and personal identity, it is striking that he was most gripped by questions about how to live in the world – summed up, for him, in the dilemma between marriage and monasticism. We now call these 'existential questions'. We probably owe to Kierkegaard the very concepts of an existential question, and an existential crisis, although existentialism did not emerge as a recognisable philosophical movement until the mid-twentieth century.

In 1844 Kierkegaard turned away from the theme of romantic love to write two ground-breaking theological works: *Philosophical Fragments* and *The Concept of Anxiety*. Unlike his earlier published books, these are academic treatises. *Philosophical Fragments* argues that the Church's teaching that the eternal God became incarnate in the historical Jesus is an 'absolute paradox', which human reason cannot penetrate. Faced with this doctrine, our rational minds must either reject it, or surrender before it. Here again, Kierkegaard launched a philosophical polemic against his contemporaries who sought to rationalise Christian faith, either by marshalling historical evidence in support of the Incarnation, or by showing that it made logical sense. In the *Concept of Anxiety* his analysis is more recognisably 'existential', though the subject of this treatise is the doctrine of original sin. Contrary to the orthodox position, taught by Augustine, that human beings inherit sinfulness biologically from Adam, who himself fell into sin through his free choice to disobey God, Kierkegaard suggested that every sin, like Adam's first sin, arises in freedom. Displaying acute psychological insight, he argued that anxiety is a ubiquitous response to the consciousness of our own freedom – and that sin constantly re-emerges in our attempts to flee this anxiety.

Kierkegaard returned to the story of his broken engagement in the voluminous *Stages on Life's Way* (1845), which reprised the complex literary strategies as well as the subject matter of *Either/Or*. He was a compulsive writer, though he agonised about publishing his works; more large books quickly followed, including *Concluding Unscientific Postscript* (1846), *Works of Love* (1847) and *Christian Discourses* (1848). Among the most significant in its lasting impact is *The Sickness Unto Death* (1849), a philosophical diagnostic manual for lost souls.

This book explores in detail the spiritual condition of despair, defined as losing oneself through turning away from God. Here Kierkegaard argued that human beings are not just bodies and minds, but spiritual beings, related to a higher power – yet we all face the task of becoming ourselves.

'Becoming oneself' is a slippery and paradoxical idea. For Kierkegaard, it means consciously living out one's dependence on God, by becoming aware of this reality instead of denying it:

> There is so much talk about wasting a life, but only that person's life was wasted who went on living so deceived by life's joys or its sorrows that he never became decisively and eternally conscious as spirit, as a self – or, what amounts to the same thing, never became aware in the deepest sense that there is a God and that he, he himself, exists before this God – an infinite benefaction that is never to be gained except through despair.

Most people, Kierkegaard observed, lose themselves in this world without even realising it, and without anyone else noticing. Indeed, this spiritual carelessness can appear to be the ease of a happy, successful life:

Just by losing himself in this way, such a man has gained an increasing capacity for going along superbly in business and social life, for making a great success in the world. Here there is no delay, no difficulty with his self and its infinite movements; he is as smooth as a rolling stone, as *courant* as a circulating coin. He is so far from being regarded as a person in despair that he is just what a human being is supposed to be.

According to Kierkegaard, despair is a blessing, for it is the sign of a human being's connection to God, his highest possibility. Yet it is also a curse, for the depth of the human soul is measured by the intensity of its suffering.

All these ideas – about anxiety and despair, the Incarnation and original sin, faith and ethics – influenced philosophy and theology through the twentieth century, and they continue to be debated today. Perhaps even more significant, however, is Kierkegaard's distinctive philosophical style, reflecting the way his intellectual work drew directly from his personal experience. We glimpse the extraordinary power of his thinking in a heartfelt letter from an unknown reader, who wrote to him in 1851 after hearing him deliver a sermon in the Citadel Church by Copenhagen's harbour – one of a handful of occasions on which he preached in a church.

'From the very outset when you began to publish your pseudonymous works', this woman wrote:

> I have pricked up my ears and listened lest I
> should miss any sound, even the faintest, of these
> magnificent harmonies, for everything resounded
> in my heart. This was what needed to be said –
> here I found answers to all my questions; nothing
> was omitted of that which interested me most
> profoundly ... I doubt that there is a single string
> in the human heart that you do not know how to
> pluck, any recess that you have not penetrated ...
> I am never lonely, even when I am by myself for
> long periods of time, provided only that I have
> the company of these books, for they are, of all
> books, those that most closely resemble the
> company of a living person.

Clare Carlisle is Professor of Philosophy at King's College London. Her biography, Philosopher of the Heart: The Restless Life of Søren Kierkegaard, *was published in 2019.*

Gottfried Wilhelm Leibniz

by Tim Crane

Voltaire's *Candide* (1759) tells the story of its young protagonist, who suffers terribly through no fault of his own, yet accepts it all with equanimity by employing the philosophy of his teacher, the learned Dr Pangloss. Pangloss argues, from apparently sound philosophical principles, that our world is the best world possible, and that since 'all is for the best in the best of all possible worlds', everything that happens in this world must be for the best.

Candide observes the horrors of warfare, torture, rape, slavery and imprisonment, the Lisbon earthquake of 1755, and many other terrible things. He frequently puzzles over Pangloss's doctrine: 'I am the best man in the world, and yet I have already killed three men, and of these three, two were priests'. Pangloss himself does not escape suffering: he catches syphilis and is hanged for his beliefs (though miraculously survives due to the incompetence of the hangman).

Pangloss (who 'taught the metaphysico-theologo-cosmolo-nigology') is generally believed to be a parody of Gottfried Wilhelm Leibniz (1646–1716). Leibniz is, without question, one of the greatest thinkers in the western philosophical canon. In addition to his extraordinary philosophical system, he made fundamental contributions to mathematics (most notably the invention of the calculus) and physics. In the twentieth century, the English philosopher C. D. Broad described Leibniz as 'probably the most universal genius that there had ever been in Europe'.

Unlike the vague and unworldly Pangloss, Leibniz was a sophisticated cosmopolitan, who worked as a diplomat, courtier and archivist for the Electors of Mainz and Hannover. He experimented with various technical inventions, including a scheme to drain water from mines using wind power, and founded various academies in St Petersburg, Vienna and Berlin (the last is still in existence). He was known for his good company and charm. Elisabeth Charlotte, Duchess of Orléans, famously said of him that 'it is so rare for intellectuals to be smartly dressed, and not to smell, and to understand jokes'.

And unlike, for example, John Locke or Immanuel Kant, Leibniz never held a university position. He published only one substantial philosophical book in his lifetime, the *Theodicy* (1710). Most of his philosophy survives in a series of short, often condensed, argumentative outlines of his system, in letters or short essays.

Yet a parody would be worthless if it did not in some way resemble its target. And, despite their dissimilarities, Dr Pangloss does also resemble Leibniz – at least in his view that our world is the best of all possible worlds. The question raised by Voltaire's novella is how this could possibly be a reasonable thing to believe, given the manifest horrors of this world. This is one way of expressing what is known as the 'problem of evil': how is the existence of evil (the term covering both wicked deeds and natural disasters) compatible with the existence of God? God comes into the picture for Leibniz since his argument that our world is the best is based on three ideas: that God created the world, that He is omniscient, and that He must always choose the best.

That's the problem for Leibniz. An additional problem for contemporary readers is to understand how someone so undeniably brilliant as Leibniz could have committed himself to such a view.

To find the answer, we need to learn a little bit about Leibniz's philosophical system. Bertrand Russell once said that 'the true philosophic spirit' requires 'following wherever the argument may lead'. In reality, not all true philosophers end up doing this. Rather than accepting all the straightforward consequences of their assumptions, they will often qualify their view, or discern ambiguities, or add something which amounts to saying: 'OK, well, you know what I am getting at ...'

René Descartes, for example, first defined his central notion of 'substance' (more below) as that which is capable of existing independently of all other things. But since on Descartes's world-view, everything depends on God, only God is a substance in this sense. So he back-pedals and distinguishes between substance 'strictly speaking' (where God is the only substance), and 'created substances' (of which human minds and matter are examples). We know what he is getting at, but he is not exactly following wherever his argument is leading.

Leibniz, however, conforms to Russell's description of the 'philosophic spirit'. Although his philosophical system is highly abstract and obscure – Russell himself called it a 'fantastic fairy tale' – it is systematically derived from a few simple principles, the consequences of which he follows through rigorously. As with many philosophers of his era, God was central to Leibniz's system, and it is impossible to understand it without understanding the place occupied by God.

But before getting on to God, we should first consider two less theological ideas which are at the core of Leibniz's system: the idea of substance, and the Principle of Sufficient Reason.

'Substance' in its philosophical sense does not have its everyday meaning (i.e. *stuff*). Rather, a substance is a fundamental being. This idea, derived originally from Aristotle, was central to many of the philosophers of this period, especially the great 'rationalist' philosophers, of whom Leibniz, Descartes and Baruch Spinoza are the most distinguished examples. (Rationalists are those who believe that the ultimate basis of our knowledge is reason, not the experience of our senses.)

As just noted, Descartes defined a substance as something capable of independent existence, and ended up with the 'dualist' view that there are two kinds of substance, mental and physical. Spinoza employed a similar definition, ending up with the more consistent ('monist') view that there is only one substance, which we could call *God* or *Nature*.

Leibniz started in a different place. His idea of substance had two central aspects. The first is that substances – fundamental beings – must be simple: they can have no parts. Leibniz argued, not entirely convincingly, that 'there must be simple substances everywhere, because, without simples, there would be no composites'. The second aspect is that each substance has a 'complete notion' that includes everything that ever happens to it, or is true of it. The complete notion 'defines' each substance: it says what makes each substance distinct from all the others. Leibniz's paradigmatic examples of substances are human souls, since he believed that they have no parts. But if Leibniz's second aspect is true, then how can we make sense of the idea that a particular substance, a fundamental thing, might have been different from the way it actually is? Leibniz's view seems to imply that no substance could have been different from what it is. But this seems to imply that all truths about the world are *necessary*, that nothing is *contingent*. And this threatens a very basic distinction in our thinking.

We all accept that some truths are necessary. Mathematical truths, for example, could not have been otherwise: 2 plus 2 could not have equalled anything other than 4. But our conception of the world also relies on the idea that many truths are contingent: that the world might have been other than it is. We speculate about how our lives might have gone if we had made different decisions. How would your life have been if you had gone to a different school, met a different partner or lived in a different country? Historians often speculate about how history might have turned out if some event had not happened; for example, how would things have been different if Julius Caesar had not invaded Britain in 55 BC?

These speculations make perfectly good sense to us. But they presuppose that much of history is contingent: that it might have been otherwise from the way it actually is. However, if it is part of the complete notion of Caesar that he invaded Britain in 55 BC, then it is not possible for Caesar himself not to have done that. If he had not done it, he would not have been Caesar.

One problem for Leibniz's philosophy, then, is that it seems to make all truths necessary. In *Candide*, Pangloss happily accepted that 'things could not be otherwise than what they were'. But few are willing to join him in this. And a further consequence seems to be that human freedom is impossible. For a person to act freely, it must be possible for them to have done otherwise than they did; freedom requires contingency. No contingency, no freedom.

The second central idea in Leibniz's system is the Principle of Sufficient Reason. This is the apparently innocuous claim that when something is true, there is always a reason *why* it is true rather than not. A special case of this is that whenever something happens, there must be a reason why it happens rather than not. Sometimes these reasons are causes of why something happens, but sometimes not – not all reasons are causes. The reason why 2 plus 2 is 4 is not the cause of why 2 plus 2 is 4 (in fact, this is an idea that makes little sense).

Leibniz describes God creating the world as God choosing to actualise one among an infinity of 'possible worlds'. According to the Principle of Sufficient Reason, God must then have had a reason to actualise this world rather than any other. Now, since God is perfectly good, his reason for choosing to actualise this world must have been a morally good reason. If God could have created a better world, he would have done so: it would be incompatible with God's goodness not to bring the best possible world into existence. So the world he did actually create must be the best world he could have created: this world is the best of all possible worlds.

This simple line of reasoning also seems to lead to the conclusion that things could not have been otherwise. For if God must always choose the best, among all the possible worlds, how could any other world have been made? It looks again as if contingency is impossible. Notice that this second (theological) source of the problem of contingency is independent of the first source: even if Leibniz's conception of substance is ignored, then we could still raise the problem of how God could have created a world other than the one he did create.

Leibniz answered these questions with a very sophisticated account of contingency. He distinguished truths which are a necessary consequence of God's free choice, from those truths which are necessary *in themselves*. Truths which are a consequence of God's free choice may be 'possible in their own nature', by which he means they 'do not imply a contradiction in themselves'. But they could still then be necessary, given God's choice.

Leibniz marks out those truths which are possible in themselves – in other words, those which are contingently true – as those that do not involve a logical contradiction. 'Caesar invaded Britain' is one such. And so is 'Caesar did not invade Britain' – both of these involve no contradiction 'in themselves'. But only one of these propositions is true – that Caesar invaded Britain – because it is a necessary consequence of God's free choice of this world. We can call this, then, a proposition that is contingent in itself.

What, then, is the difference between truths that are necessary in themselves, and truths that are contingent in themselves? Truths that are necessary in themselves – e.g. all triangles are trilaterals – can be given a finite logical demonstration. In this example, the connection between the concept of triangularity and the concept of trilaterality is easy for our finite minds to prove or demonstrate. The purely logical demonstration of other truths, by contrast, will often have an infinite number of steps, since it will (according to Leibniz) involve the infinity of truths about the world. When a true proposition lacks a finite logical demonstration, Leibniz says that the proposition is contingent.

God's mind is infinite in scope, and so God can logically deduce any truth from any other, even if the deduction would take an infinite number of steps. Our minds are finite, however, and so there are some truths that cannot be deduced by our reason alone, but which we have to know in other ways (for example, by our senses). These truths are the contingent truths, and the truths which we can deduce by logical demonstration alone are the necessary truths.

In order to see why this is not ad hoc or arbitrary, we need a change of perspective. Leibniz is trying to give a *reduction* of the idea of contingency: an explanation of it in other terms. These days we are inclined to take contingency as a primitive, unexplained starting point in philosophy. Influenced by the broadly empiricist outlook of natural science, we tend to see the natural world as something that just 'happens' to be there – contingently, even accidentally, existing. Against this background, necessary truth (e.g. mathematics, logic) is what needs explaining, not contingent truth.

Leibniz takes a very different view. For him contingency is neither primitive nor without need of explanation. For Leibniz, the starting points are the notion of substance, the Principle of Sufficient Reason, and the existence and nature of God. Given these principles, contingency is problematic. So Leibniz attempts to account for it in other terms.

Let's return to the problem of evil. Since this is the best of all possible worlds, how can God allow evil to exist? Leibniz's worry here is not that this provides an argument against the existence of God, which was not up for question in Leibniz's system. It's rather that the existence of evil challenges his conception of God, and of God's holiness. So how does Leibniz deal with this problem?

First, for Leibniz, the fact that the world is the best of all possible worlds does not imply that it is a *perfect* world. He believed that only God could be perfect, so anything that is distinct from God must be imperfect in certain ways. So if we are to properly distinguish between God and the world, we must allow that the world is imperfect. The world is necessarily bounded or limited. To deny this is to lose the distinction between God and the world (this was Spinoza's mistake, identifying the world, or nature, with God).

For Leibniz, God is an infinite substance; he is also perfect. These ideas are related: if something is finite, it is limited in some way. Since God is 'incapable of limits' and therefore contains 'as much reality as possible', it follows that he is perfect, since perfection 'is nothing but the total amount of positive reality ... leaving aside the limitations or boundaries of things which have them'.

It is one thing to accept that the world must be imperfect – but why must it be as imperfect as it is? Perhaps we can accept that there should be some 'evil' in the world – but why so much? To understand Leibniz's position here, let's return to his explanation of contingency.

For Leibniz, a truth is contingent when its denial is not a contradiction that can be demonstrated in a finite number of steps. We cannot prove that 'Julius Caesar did not invade Britain' is a contradiction. But this is a fact of our intellectual limitations. God's understanding is unlimited, and because of this God can prove that it is a contradiction.

A similar explanation applies to the problem of evil. The world is imperfect, but we cannot understand the specific ways in which it has to be imperfect. Only God can fully understand this. Because of what Leibniz called 'the interconnectedness of things', even the most egregious wrong has a place in the best of all possible worlds. The fact that we cannot understand this is something we have to come to terms with.

But we might still ask: how can God let this happen? Why can't God make people better? According to Leibniz, God does not make people act in an evil way; but he discovers, because of his omniscience, what the consequences of their possible actions will be. These truths about how people would act function as 'limitations' on the perfection of the world. God can understand all these things, but we cannot.

On this understanding of Leibniz's views, the problem of evil is, like the problem of contingency, ultimately an epistemological problem, a problem about our knowledge, deriving from the contrast between a perfect God and his imperfect creations. The contrast between necessary and contingent truth is understood in terms of the difference between what we can prove, in a finite number of steps, and what God can prove. Analogously, the manifest tension between the existence of evil and the claim that this is the best of all possible worlds is explained in terms of God's perfection and our inability to understand the connections between things.

This is a highly abstract, metaphysical solution of the problem of evil, which may seem very distant from the concrete questions facing believers when they encounter the horrors of reality. Yet our ignorance in the face of God's omniscience and majesty is also a thread in the Christian apologetic tradition. In the Book of Job, for example, God responds to Job's complaints by speaking to him out of the whirlwind: 'Where were you when I laid the foundations of the earth?' Job responds by acknowledging his ignorance. But God gives Job no understanding of why things have happened to him as they have; Job must simply accept it. Which in the end, like Candide, he does.

Tim Crane is Professor of Philosophy at the Central European University.

Niccolò Machiavelli

by William J. Connell

At first glance, Niccolò Machiavelli's pessimistic characterisation of human nature seems to understand
mankind as living in a fallen or sinful state; we are all, he
wrote, 'ungrateful, changeable, pretenders and dissem-
blers, avoiders of dangers, and desirous of gain'. But
although Machiavelli (1469–1527) found wickedness in
the race of man, he differed from contemporaries like
Luther in attributing it not to Adam and Eve's eating fruit
from the Tree of Knowledge of Good and Evil (and hence
their sexual intimacy), but instead to 'the first violent
death': the killing of Abel by Cain. In a remarkable poem,
'On Ambition', Machiavelli imagines how, although Adam
and Eve were sent out from the Garden of Eden for diso-
beying the divine commandment, they continued to
lead, 'joyously in a humble home ... a sweet and tranquil
life'. Alas, to disturb this pleasant state, the poem
explains, a hidden, baleful astral power sent Furies to

poison the mind of Cain against Abel. And so, beginning from the crime of brother against brother, the human character became infected. From what had been their happy primitive existence, people became 'insatiable, treacherous, malignant, iniquitous, impetuous, and unbridled'. The real original sin, inherited and ever-present, had nothing to do with knowledge or sexual desire. It resided in the possibility of wilfully putting another human being to death.

In the western intellectual tradition, Machiavelli foreshadowed, and in some respects initiated, a key project of the Enlightenment. His advice to rulers and to the founders of regimes was to take the fallen nature of mankind as a given and, rather than seek to correct it or wish it otherwise, to build on it positively. In Machiavelli's writings there began a transformation, central to modern political thought, by which features like acquisitiveness would be legitimised as the pursuit of happiness, and the telling of falsehoods permitted (save in certain legal contexts) as an exercise of free speech.

The Machiavelli were one of twenty or so Guelf families in Florence that dominated the city's politics from the late thirteenth century. Bernardo Machiavelli, Niccolò's father, was born out of wedlock and orphaned soon after, but he was raised and accepted by the family and trained as a lawyer, although he appears not to have practised law. Bernardo saw to it that his son received a humanist education, and although his father's illegitimate birth meant he could not aspire to the city's highest offices, in 1498, in the political aftermath of the execution of the prophetic friar Girolamo Savonarola, Niccolò Machiavelli was appointed Florence's Second Chancellor (with responsibility for territorial affairs) and Secretary to the Ten of War (the council responsible for military and foreign affairs). Service in legations to Popes Alexander VI and Julius II, Cesare Borgia, Louis XII of France and Emperor Maximilian I, as well as to neighbouring Italian states, afforded him rich experiences on which he would draw in his later writings.

In 1512, with the collapse of a republican government in Florence and the return of the exiled Medici family, Machiavelli was cashiered and forbidden to leave Florentine territory. In February 1513, when a plot against the Medici was discovered, Machiavelli's name surfaced, and he was arrested and tortured, although he proclaimed his innocence and there is no evidence he was involved in the conspiracy. Freed from prison in March 1513 thanks to an amnesty proclaimed after the election of a Florentine as pope (Giovanni de' Medici, who became Leo X), Machiavelli sought employment with the Medici, unsuccessfully at first. At this time he wrote his most famous work, *The Prince* (1513–1515), while his *Discourses on Livy* (1514–1517) were written mostly during the subsequent period in which

Machiavelli frequented a literary and philosophical circle that met in gardens decorated with ancient statuary that belonged to the Rucellai family. The Rucellai Gardens provided the setting of the dialogue in his next book, *The Art of War* (published in 1521). Machiavelli's famous play, *Mandragola* is likely to have been written in this period as well. In his last years Machiavelli performed various, largely military functions in service to the Medici papacy, and seems to have been active in Roman literary circles. He died in 1527, shortly after the Sack of Rome by Imperial forces and the restoration in Florence of a republican government that again exiled the Medici who were then employing him.

Certain themes are present throughout all of Machiavelli's writings: the deprecation of human nature; the need to know how to be 'not good'; an instrumental view of religion; the gullibility but also the common sense of the masses; the variability of fortune; a positive assessment of class conflict; the necessity of severity and speed in establishing new regimes. The works on which his reputation rests today, where these themes are most on display, are *The Prince* and the *Discourses on Livy*.

The Prince is a relatively brief treatise comprising twenty-six chapters and a dedicatory letter. Although written with the new pope, Leo X, in mind, Machiavelli originally intended to dedicate the work to the pope's younger brother, Giuliano de' Medici (1479–1516), in the hope of securing a position as minister or secretary in what was anticipated to be a new principality in northern Italy. This partly explains the prominence with which Machiavelli treats Cesare Borgia's project of state-building in Romagna. An immediate purpose of the work was thus to offer advice for the creation of a new and lasting state in an unruly and faction-prone Italian region. Yet from the outset Machiavelli advertised his work as a general treatise 'On Principalities' (the original title was *De Principatibus*), and the matter discussed is often universal in nature. When, in 1515, a planned appointment under Giuliano was vetoed, Machiavelli dedicated *The Prince* instead to the ascendant *de facto* ruler of Florence, the pope's nephew, Lorenzo de' Medici the Younger (1492–1519). Since the previously planned dedication to Giuliano, with a view to his princely state, had been abandoned, the work was read thereafter as an intended roadmap for Lorenzo, the actual dedicatee, to consolidate princely power in traditionally republican Florence. It is unlikely that Machiavelli had that end in mind, as other writings show he was attached to the city's republican institutions. Yet his book offered what he believed to be useful lessons in effective rulership that he thought applicable anywhere. His rules, moreover, famously contradicted the precepts of the long-established genre of advice books for rulers known as 'Mirrors for princes'.

Where previous writers praised liberality, Machiavelli urged liberality with the wealth of others and stinginess with one's own money. Where others urged the prince to be loved rather than feared, Machiavelli concluded it was better to be feared since being loved requires the consent of others, while only one's own will is required to impose fear. Other writers wanted princes to keep their word, but Machiavelli praised the princes who knew 'to so spin men's brains' that they outdid the ones who were sincere. As he wrote in one especially pungent passage:

> There is such a distance from how one lives to how one ought to live that he who abandons what is done for what ought to be done learns what will ruin him rather than what will save him, since a man who would wish to make a career of being good in every detail must come to ruin among so many who are not good. Hence it is necessary for a prince, if he wishes to maintain himself, to learn to be able to be *not* good, and to use this faculty, and to not use it, according to necessity.

The sarcasm sometimes verges on satire, but the intent is clear. The condemnation of tyrants that was customary since classical times in political treatises of this kind was omitted by Machiavelli, who instead referred only to 'new princes'. Possibly he understood that historically the Greek word '*turannos*' meant 'new ruler' (as in the *Oedipus tyrannus* of Sophocles), and that only with the passage of time did the label attach to cruel usurpers. The book's concluding chapter, an 'Exhortation' to Lorenzo and the Medici to take charge of Italy so as to reclaim her liberty from foreign powers ('the barbarians'), reprises an idea and slogan of Pope Julius II, and it charges the new prince with a patriotic and ennobling task that would have required harsh measures – creating an army, exacting revenues, extinguishing factious malcontents – in order to succeed.

The *Discourses on Livy* is Machiavelli's longest work and his most considered. It is a volume about republics that he thought complementary with *The Prince*, but also more valuable. When first published in 1531 it was the first text in a posthumously issued three-volume set of Machiavelli's writings. According to the full title (*Discorsi sopra la prima deca di Tito Livio*) it comprised 'discourses' (essays) on the first ten books, or 'decade', of Livy's monumental Roman history, although in reality the subject matter extended to all Roman history and to much else as well, including events contemporary with Machiavelli. Curiously, the text gives the appearance of being provisional or incomplete, and possibly it is. There is no formal conclusion to the work as a whole, and unlike Books I and II, the third and final book lacks a preface and there is no formal conclusion. Surprisingly, as Leo Strauss once pointed out, the number of 'discourses' in the three books (sixty, thirty-three and forty-nine) totals 142, which is precisely the number of the books comprised in Livy's full history (which survives only in part). Yet a very good friend of the author, Francesco Guicciardini, read a version in manuscript in 1529–30 – thus after Machiavelli's death in 1527, but before the book's 1531 publication – whose chapters were differently numbered and arranged. There is thus likely to have been some editorial adjustment of the chapters after Machiavelli's death and before publication, but whether or not that followed any precise wishes of his we do not know.

A desire for revision may have led Machiavelli to neglect to publish *The Discourses* while he lived, but the book also contained passages critical of the Church and the Christian religion that might easily have got him into trouble with ecclesiastical authorities. To cite one instance only, Machiavelli criticises Christianity for having 'rendered the world weak, and given it in prey to wicked men, who are able to manipulate it securely, since mankind, in order to go to Heaven, thinks how to endure the beatings they receive, rather than how to avenge them'.

The book's treatment of republicanism was especially consequential. Europe in Machiavelli's day was developing a system of national monarchies in which republicanism was losing its footing. Even in Italy, many major city states evolved from medieval communes into territorial principalities, so that after 1560 the only important republics were Venice, Genoa and Lucca. Yet Machiavelli's *Discourses*, with its analysis and praise of the Roman Republic, argued for the superiority of republican government. But the kind of regime he advocated differed from the republics described by ancient and medieval writers. Machiavelli's explanation of the greatness of Rome was novel. The Florentine broke with earlier writers' endorsement, traditional in political thought, of the *concordia ordinum*, Cicero's term for the harmony of the social orders that was believed vital to the state's success. Machiavelli argued instead that it was a good thing to have ongoing competition between a republic's patricians and its people. To be sure there would be 'tumults', but these offered a way for the people to check oligarchic tendencies among the patricians. Machiavelli was thus more democratic than previous republican theorists. And the worst instincts of the populace, he believed, could be managed by manipulating its religious beliefs and by requiring military service. Machiavelli's ideal republic was expansive, like Rome, rather than static and self-contained. Ancient theorists had imagined that the purpose of the republic was to promote the virtue of its citizens, but for

Machiavelli its goal (*'fine'* in Italian) was 'acquisition' – an idea that accorded with his revisionist anthropology, since, as he stated in *The Prince*, 'It is a thing truly very natural and ordinary to desire to acquire'. Although Machiavelli had no experience in trade, and his works denied commerce a major role, the principles underlying his republicanism were compatible with commerce in ways that classical doctrine and Christian dogma were not.

By embracing possessiveness, competition between the classes, salutary violence and a growing state, Machiavelli transformed western political thought. He claimed, as he put it, empirically 'to go after the effectual truth of the matter', as opposed to its 'imagination'. In truth, Machiavelli was not immune from idealism. Yet, as one reads him, one often feels he describes today's world, albeit in the guise of ancient Rome or his own beloved Florence.

William J. Connell is Professor of History and holder of the La Motta Endowed Chair in Italian Studies at Seton Hall University.

John Stuart Mill

by Christopher Macleod

John Stuart Mill (1806–1873), perhaps the most consequential English-speaking philosopher of the nineteenth
century, is today best remembered as the author of *On
Liberty* (1859). The work is, he notes, a 'kind of philosophic textbook of a single truth' – one in which he
argues that there should be no interference with the
thought, speech or action of any individual except on the
grounds of the prevention of harm to others. That prohi-
bition applies to legislative or state action, but also to
those informal modes of coercion that can be practised
by society itself. And the ban is total. 'Over himself, over
his own body and mind, the individual is sovereign.'
Though occasionally challenged by the collectivist left,
the position Mill argues for has become orthodoxy in
modern Anglo-American political thought.

But while liberalism *itself* remains pre-eminent, Mill's
particular arguments for the position have fallen out of

sight in recent discussions. In contrast to many present-day thinkers, Mill's defence of liberal principles is historical and local – not abstract and universal. Whereas the prevailing wisdom maintains that individuals possess certain rights to free speech and action simply by virtue of their status as human beings, Mill was suspicious of that claim. As a robust naturalist – one who believed only in those objects discovered by observation or the methods of empirical science – Mill could not accept the idea of rights which attach to every human being but were wholly imperceptible to the senses. Nor could he agree with those who, like the United States' Founding Fathers, held that our possession of certain unalienable rights was 'self-evident'. If such rights *were* self-evident, he notes, there would hardly be so much disagreement about them.

Mill's argument for the principle of liberty is based on an observation about the conditions most conducive to flourishing in societies that have reached a certain level of civilisation. Given the level of moral and intellectual cultivation achieved in western Europe – modest, Mill suggests, but not insignificant – a robust atmosphere of freedom is indispensable for the advancement of knowledge and the achievement of happiness. In the modern era, individuals are the best judges of their own good, and are best equipped to appreciate and understand the truth only when they hear all sides of an argument. It is

this which justifies an absolute protection of free speech
and self-regarding action – not our possession of some
abstract entitlement to non-interference.

The argument, we should note, is utilitarian in orien-
tation. It appeals to a claim about the conditions that will
lead to overall happiness, given how human beings now
are. This mode of argument is, of course, double-edged
– for in the process of offering a vindication of liberal
rights here and now, it also implies that, where different
circumstances obtain, those same liberties might not be
justified. While individuals in 'civilised' societies thrive in
an atmosphere that protects rights of freedom, for
nations that belong to a 'barbarous state' the best thing
would be 'obedience to an Akbar or a Charlemagne, if
they are so fortunate as to find one'. The suggestion that
liberal rights are suitable only for societies that have
reached a certain level of development is likely to strike
us as blinkered – and it is certainly true that we should
be suspicious of the Victorian confidence with which Mill
categorises entire nations as 'barbarous' or 'civilised'.
But the underlying thought – that one and the same set
of norms might not have the same effects if embedded in
different settings – does have the virtue of being attentive to the reality of the historical emergence of liberal
societies.

The utilitarianism that Mill deployed in arguing for the
value of freedom was, primarily, a product of his

upbringing in the Enlightenment tradition of Jeremy Bentham. A generation earlier, Bentham had proposed what he termed 'the greatest happiness principle' – that actions or policies should be judged moral to the extent that they contribute to the total sum of pleasure in the world – and applied it enthusiastically to criticise the archaic laws and religious beliefs of eighteenth-century England. With Enlightenment optimism, Bentham declared that all that was necessary to unleash human potential was to sweep away corrupted institutions and replace them with ones designed to maximise happiness.

Mill agreed with Bentham's criticisms of eighteenth-century England, which of course took place in the context of a broader European deconstruction of the *ancien régime*. In his early twenties, however, Mill had been heavily influenced by the Romantic tradition, absorbing the writings of William Wordsworth, Samuel Taylor Coleridge and Thomas Carlyle. This work left him feeling that, although Bentham had been right in his endorsement of the greatest happiness principle, like the French *philosophes* his understanding of human nature, and therefore his application of that principle, had been naive. 'He knew no dejection, no heaviness of heart', Mill commented. 'He never felt life a sore and a weary burthen. He was a boy to the last.' Mill's goal would be to reconcile the insights of Bentham with the nineteenth-century poets. This would, in practice, amount to nothing less than the attempt to reconcile the Enlightenment and Romantic visions of man. 'Whoever could master the premises and combine the methods of both', he thought, 'would possess the entire English philosophy of their age.'

Mill's effort to combine Enlightenment and Romantic thought reached into every area of his philosophy. The Enlightenment tradition, broadly speaking, had endorsed a scientific world-view in which man was wholly governed by the causal regularities observable in nature. Mill thought this view quite correct – but he also felt keenly the Romantic concern that this 'mechanical philosophy' threatened to render human beings passive. If man was subject to invariable laws, how could he be capable of *self*-guided action? Mill's solution was to maintain that human beings were subject to deterministic laws, but to point to their ability to influence their own character. Individuals' actions might be solely a product of their character and environment, but they could act to progressively alter their characters and thereby control their future actions if they so desired. Indeed, increased knowledge of the deterministic laws of psychology would – by revealing the mechanisms of the formation of character – allow us to better understand how to cultivate strong-willed individuals capable of self-governance. 'Out of mechanical premises', he wrote to Carlyle, 'I elicit dynamical conclusions.'

Mill's dynamic view of man led him, as a utilitarian, to prize those forms of happiness involving self-development and genuine engagement with the world. Such a conception of utility was at the root of his arguments for liberty. Whereas Bentham had seen all pleasures as on a par – 'prejudice apart, the game of push-pin', he had written, with reference to a children's game of the period, 'is of equal value with the arts and sciences of music and poetry' – Mill viewed pleasures actively taken in the world as more valuable than those received passively. Such 'higher' pleasures resulted from the self-directed use of our distinctively human capacities, and were to be preferred over the 'lower' pleasures which involved merely the use of our animal faculties. The former variety included, he thought, the pleasures of intellectual and aesthetic involvement. The influence of the Romantics was again significant.

Mill's reflections on the superiority of some forms of pleasure took place in the context of society trying quickly to come to terms with its own changing economic and social identity. The Industrial Revolution and the Great Reform Act of 1832 had ushered in a new era in Great Britain – and both foretold further, even more dramatic changes. Such developments were, in Mill's view, inevitable. Wealth, education, status and therefore power, he held, were amassing with a socially and politically dominant middle class, whose shared commercial traits and interests dictated equality as the emerging rule. The 'irresistible tendency to equality of conditions' would soon impact all aspects of human life.

Most directly, he anticipated, these changes would impact structures of governance. In the context of the growth of equality, various existing forms of political inequality stood out all the more clearly – in particular, the denial of the vote to women – and the time was therefore ripe to dismantle such practices of discrimination. Mill argued vigorously, both as a philosopher and as a Member of Parliament, for the enfranchisement of women. The denial of the vote to women not only meant that their interests were unrepresented in the national political conversation, but also that they were denied access to the important goods of political participation. '[A]n equal right to be heard – to have a share in influencing the affairs of the country – to be consulted, to be spoken to, and to have agreements and considerations turning upon politics addressed to one – tended to elevate and educate.' Such goods, he argued, were pivotal to leading a happy life, and should be made available to all.

Witnessing the progress of democratic sentiments throughout the nineteenth century, though, Mill also worried deeply about the levelling effects that might result from these changes: with the growth of equality, he thought, came a suspicion of the superior and a veneration of the average. Deference to the majority on political matters, Mill held, made deference to the majority on questions of value and the intellect more likely – and this could lead to mediocrity and the debasement of high ideals. With democracy, then, came the serious danger of cultural decline. That concern seemed to become all the more real as the effects of industrial capitalism gradually played out, and it was shared by other thinkers of the period: most prominently, of course, Friedrich Nietzsche.

Mill ultimately remained optimistic about the possibility of maintaining high culture in conditions of equality, however. 'It is the honour and glory of the average man', he wrote, 'that he can respond internally to wise and noble things, and be led to them with his eyes open.' He was conscious that effort is required to preserve this ability – that the human facility to discriminate the true and valuable from the merely widespread and popular is not natural, innate or guaranteed. Only by education, he suggested, could that ability be cultivated in a democracy and passed on to future generations. The problem, of course, would become whether democratic society's commitment to education could be sufficiently self-sustaining to guard against the descent into populism. That is a question that remains very much with us.

Christopher Macleod is a Professor of Philosophy at Lancaster University, and co-editor of A Companion to Mill, *2017.*

Iris Murdoch

by Anil Gomes

Was Iris Murdoch (1919–1999) a novelistic philosopher, or a philosophical novelist? For the majority of her career, she was the latter: an ex-philosophy don who became an internationally recognised novelist. And if her fiction sometimes had its detractors – Martin Amis once commented that in the Murdochian paradigm the men all have names like Hilary and Julian, while the women all have names like Julian and Hilary – that never prevented her sometimes strange and often remarkable novels from capturing and maintaining readers' affection.

But before she was a novelist, she was a philosopher: first, as a student of Classics at Somerville College, Oxford, and later as a Tutorial Fellow in Philosophy at St Anne's College, Oxford. At Somerville she was part of a generation of distinctive philosophers: Iris Murdoch, Philippa Foot and Mary Midgley all took their final exams in 1942; Elizabeth Anscombe had taken hers at St Hugh's the previous year. These individual and independent intellects were formed in an atmosphere of ongoing conversation – one from which, Mary Midgley noted, the men were absent, most of them being away at the war.

Murdoch's career seems to have been brilliant from the start. She was a presence in Oxford – in campaigns, in arguments, at parties – and when she left to work in the civil service, her intense friendship with Foot continued, the two of them sharing a small flat in London, listening out for German bombs. When the war finished, she worked with the United Nations Relief and Rehabilitation Administration, travelling across Europe and seeing for herself the destruction of the war. She met Jean-Paul Sartre in Brussels, spent some time in Cambridge as a student, talking with Ludwig Wittgenstein and his students, and then, in 1948, was elected to a Fellowship at St Anne's, only six years after completing her final exams.

A story has built up, perhaps prompted by her later work, about Murdoch's intellectual isolation in Oxford at this time. This is a mistake. She gave talks at the Aristotelian Society, debated with the renowned Oxford philosopher Gilbert Ryle, and was among the esteemed British philosophers included in a BBC series on the nature of metaphysics. She was, in short, a central part of the Oxford philosophy scene, with all that it entailed.

So where has the story of isolation come from? It is true that Murdoch's interests gradually drifted away from the mainstream of Oxford philosophy. Or, rather, that there was a slow shift in the idiom with which she learned to express her philosophical sensitivities, together with a realignment of her reference points. Her book *Sartre* (1953) – published a year before her first novel *Under the Net* (1954) – was well received, as were her interventions on behaviourism, on the nature of theory, on Kant's view of the sublime. But it was her opposition to the dominant forms of moral philosophy that would lead to her most important and revolutionary work.

At this point, Murdoch was withdrawing from Oxford, terminating the university part of her lectureship in 1957, and leaving St Anne's completely in 1963. Her views on moral philosophy are set out in three papers published over this period, none of them in the mainstream philosophy journals where her former colleagues might have come across them, and later collected together as *The Sovereignty of Good* (1970). She presents herself throughout these essays as opposing a certain picture of moral philosophy. It is a picture, Murdoch tells us, that can be found in the work of R. M. Hare, where moral utterances are a kind of prescription; in Sartre's existentialism, where moral value is created by our undetermined choices; and in the hero of many a contemporary novel. According to this picture, moral judgements do not aim to describe how things are in the world. They cannot be true or false. Perhaps they express your emotions, perhaps they prescribe your actions, perhaps they announce your decisions – but whatever it is they do, they don't tell you how things are in the world. Morality, on this view, isn't a matter of finding out truths about the world; it is a matter of *choosing* which values guide your life.

Murdoch, Foot, Midgely and Anscombe – that wonderful generation of women philosophers – all rejected this idea of morality. The lessons of the war seemed to be that there is such a thing as getting it right or wrong, and that it mattered that one get it right. But Murdoch took the rejection much further than any of the others, and in a way which led her closer, in some guises, to Plato, and, in others, to a form of mysticism that will be familiar to anyone who has read her novels. The aim of the essays in *The Sovereignty of Good* is to replace this picture of moral life with an alternative, one that is adequate to our empirical, philosophical and moral existence.

What is this alternative picture? In contrast to her opponents, Murdoch stresses the *reality* of moral life. To acknowledge the reality of moral life is to recognise that the world contains such things as kindness, as foolishness, as mean-spiritedness. These are genuine features of reality, and someone who comes to know that some course of action would be foolish comes to know something about how things are in the world. This view is sometimes thought to be ruled out by a certain scientistic conception of the natural, one that restricts what exists to the things that feature in our best scientific theories. Such a view is too restricted, Murdoch thinks, to capture the reality of our lives – including our lives as moral agents. Goodness is sovereign, which is to say a real, if transcendent, aspect of the world.

Making sense of these ideas requires a *metaphysics* of morals, one that helps us to make peace with the existence of transcendent goodness. But if morality is to move us, we need not just a metaphysics of morals but also a moral psychology: an account of how we creatures, concrete as we are, are able to know about, and be guided by, the transcendent good. Here Murdoch aims to replace the metaphor of *choice* which dominated her opponents' work with the metaphor of *vision*. We can *look* carefully, we can *attend* to people and their situations, and when we do so, we can come to know how things are in the moral realm, to know how people have behaved, and to know what we ought to do.

This way of thinking about our capacity to be guided by the good will seem odd if you think of perception as a restricted capacity, capable of picking up on only the shapes and colours of things around us. For if that were all perception could deliver, then moral values would seem beyond its ken. But what we see depends, in part, on the kinds of concepts we have, and those with the right conceptual resources can pick up on aspects of the world to which someone else might be blind. A talented botanist, for instance, sees more in a field of wild flowers than a bored urban walker. And someone who understands kindness will see when to change a topic of conversation to avoid someone else being hurt. Perception of the moral realm requires initiation into a certain scheme of concepts, into a way of thinking about the world, and changes in conceptual schemes can enlarge, or restrict, the range of things we are able to see. For Murdoch, moral perception requires both sense *and* sensibility, and someone who possesses both can see how things ought to be.

Metaphysics and psychology come together in Murdoch's notion of *attention* – a process by which we come to see the world for what it really is. Murdoch takes the notion from her careful reading of Simone Weil, and in many ways it is her discovery of Weil that dislodges her from the comfortable ground of Oxford philosophy and gives her a language in which to express her views. Attention, for both Weil and Murdoch, is a heavily moralised notion, far removed from how it features in contemporary psychology. To attend to something is to look at it lovingly, to look at it justly. It is only by lovingly attending to things that we see them as they really are. And although I've talked about seeing *things* in general, it would be better to say that, in the moral realm, we lovingly attend to *people* – individuals with their own distinct histories and idiosyncrasies. When we attend to others, we look at them lovingly, and come to see what is required of us. Attention is our way of latching onto a moral realm that is there anyway.

Murdoch's most famous example in setting out her view is that of a mother and her daughter-in-law. Consider a mother who finds her daughter-in-law unpolished and lacking in refinement, who thinks that her son married beneath him. These views may not affect her behaviour. Perhaps the married couple live far away; perhaps the mother is perfect in her outward demeanour. Nevertheless, she may reflect on her own conventionality, on her narrow-mindedness and resolve to see her daughter-in-law more clearly. This process of *attending*, of looking lovingly and justly at her daughter-in-law, can bring her to see her daughter-in-law as she really is. This is a change in moral sensibility, and it is prompted by love.

None of this is to say that morality is easy. There are barriers to looking, often physical – when we push the needy out of sight – but psychological, too. Humans are naturally selfish creatures, and this, Murdoch thinks, is our secular version of original sin. (Murdoch took this lesson from Sigmund Freud, but someone less impressed with Freud might find the same message in Charles

Darwin.) This selfishness stops us from seeing what is there to be seen; the dear self – as Immanuel Kant puts it – gets in the way of our seeing what needs to be done. Great art can help here, providing us with an analogue for the good, and teaching us how to look carefully, to see things as they are. Looking carefully is a moral activity, and by learning how to do so, we learn to remove ourselves from view and to see the world as it really is.

Murdoch sets out this alternative picture with force and verve across the three essays in *The Sovereignty of Good*. But although moral realism is no longer neglected in contemporary philosophical discussion, Murdoch's distinctive views have not gained currency. Part of the problem is the elusive nature of her arguments, and their situation in a landscape far removed from contemporary debates. More deeply, the idea of a moral reality continues to dumbfound. For some, it smacks of a piece of supernatural mythologising. For others, it ignores the way in which our evaluations and sentiments are projected out onto the world, bringing into existence the moral landscape. And even those who are sympathetic to Murdoch's realism have struggled to make sense of the idea that love – that wonderful, particular, parochial attitude – should play a role in revealing things as they really are.

If there is a figure in the history of philosophy whom Murdoch resembles, it is Plato shorn of his hostility to art. Goodness is real, we perceive it dimly as it is reflected around us, and part of the role of moral philosophy is to improve ourselves, to get us in a position where we can liberate ourselves from fantasy and, by looking with love, see others as they really are. Here is a link between morality and fiction; both want us to recognise what can be the most difficult thing to see – the reality of other people.

So was Murdoch a novelistic philosopher or a philosophical novelist? Her philosophy, like her fiction, is populated by the varied reality of moral life: mothers who find their daughters-in-law unpolished and juvenile, concentration-camp guards who are kindly fathers. There is nothing illusory about this life: the courage of a parent and the meanness of a child are as much features of the world as cabbages and kings. And someone with a just and loving gaze can discern these aspects of moral reality just as someone with a good eye can appraise the length of a piece of timber. But being good is difficult and that dear self, our selfish ego, gets in the way. If we are to do better, we need the virtues, we need beauty, we need the development of a capacity for loving attention. It is this unselfconscious and visceral belief in the enduring power of love that is at the centre of both Murdoch's philosophy and her fiction. Her work now, as then, is a provocation, where goodness is real, and love is seeing aright.

GOOD AND EVIL

Anil Gomes is Fellow and Tutor in Philosophy, Trinity College, University of Oxford.

Friedrich Nietzsche

by Brian Leiter

The German philosopher Friedrich Nietzsche (1844–1900) pursued two main themes in his work, one now familiar, even commonplace in modernity, the other still under-appreciated, often ignored. The familiar Nietzsche is the 'existentialist' who diagnoses the most profound cultural fact about modernity: 'the death of God', or more exactly, the collapse of the possibility of reasonable belief in God. Belief in God – in transcendent meaning or purpose, dictated by a supernatural being – is now incredible, usurped by naturalistic explanations of the evolution of species, the behaviour of matter in motion, the unconscious causes of human behaviours and attitudes, indeed, by explanations of how such a bizarre belief arose in the first place. But without God or transcendent purpose, how can we withstand the terrible truths about our existence, namely, its inevitable suffering and disappointment, ending in death and the abyss of nothingness?

Nietzsche the 'existentialist' exists in tandem with an 'illiberal' Nietzsche, one who sees the collapse of theism as tied fundamentally to the untenability of the entire moral world-view of post-Christian modernity. If there is no God who deems each human to be of equal worth or possessed with an immortal soul beloved by God, then why think we all deserve equal moral consideration? And what if, as Nietzsche argues, a morality of equality – and altruism and pity for suffering – is, in fact, an obstacle to human excellence? What if being a 'moral' person makes it impossible to be Beethoven? Nietzsche's conclusion is clear: if moral equality is an obstacle to human excellence, then so much the worse for moral equality. This is the less familiar and often shockingly anti-egalitarian Nietzsche.

Nietzsche grew up in the belly of God and Christian morality. His father and his grandfathers (on both sides of his family) were Lutheran pastors, and Nietzsche himself went to university planning to study Theology. Theological studies have never had such a spectacular dropout – one who later ridiculed Luther as a 'boor' and declared himself to be the 'anti-Christian' *par excellence*. The young Nietzsche switched after one year at university to Classical Philology – the study of the texts and culture of the ancient Greek and Roman world – where he excelled, earning appointment to the University of Basel in 1869 even before completing his doctoral thesis.

He soon met the composer Richard Wagner, and was briefly a disciple, imagining that Wagner's music would redeem European culture from the ill effects of Christian morality. But his enthusiasm for Wagner subsided after a few years, as Nietzsche's mature philosophical views coalesced, and he grew disillusioned with Wagner's rabid antisemitism.

Nietzsche's classical training had educated him about ancient philosophy; the Presocratic philosophers (with their simple naturalistic world-view) were his favourites, while his disagreements with Socrates and Plato persisted throughout his work. But it was only in 1865–1866 that he came to contemporary German philosophy through Arthur Schopenhauer and, a year later, Friedrich Lange. Schopenhauer's *The World as Will and Representation* was first published in 1818, but only came to prominence decades later (and contributed to the eclipse of G. W. F. Hegel in German philosophy). It defined the central existentialist issue for Nietzsche: how can life, given that it involves continual, senseless suffering, possibly be justified? Schopenhauer offered a 'nihilistic' verdict: we would be better off dead. Nietzsche wanted to resist that conclusion, to 'affirm' life, as he often put it, to the point that we would happily will its 'eternal recurrence' (in one of his famous formulations) with all of its suffering.

Lange, by contrast, was both a neo-Kantian – an important figure in the 'back to Kant' revival in German philosophy after Hegel's eclipse – and part of the 'materialist' turn in German intellectual life, the other major reaction against Hegelian idealism after 1831. The latter trend, though familiar to philosophers today primarily by way of Ludwig Feuerbach and Karl Marx, actually received its major impetus from the dramatic developments in physiology that began in Germany in the 1830s. Materialism exploded on the German intellectual scene of the 1850s in such volumes as Ludwig Büchner's *Force and Matter*, a publishing sensation which went through multiple editions, its message that 'the researches and discoveries of modern times can no longer allow us to doubt that man, with all he has and possesses, be it mental or corporeal, is a *natural product* like all other organic beings'. (Think of Büchner as a populariser of some genuine discoveries, while also an unnuanced ideologue.) Nietzsche, who first learned of these 'German Materialists' from Lange, wrote in a letter of 1866, 'Kant, Schopenhauer, this book by Lange – I don't need anything else'.

Nietzsche soon soured on Kant, though Kant and Plato remained his most familiar philosophical opponents in his writings, and 'philosophical' isn't perhaps the right word to describe Nietzsche's critical method. For Nietzsche's writing style is anomalous in the canon of great philosophers: he writes aphoristically, polemically, lyrically and always very personally; he can be funny, sarcastic, rude, scholarly and scathing, often in the same passage. He eschews almost entirely the rationally discursive form of philosophical argumentation. In the course of examining philosophical subjects (morality, free will, knowledge), Nietzsche will invoke historical, psychological, philological and anthropological claims, and never appeal to an intuition or an *a priori* bit of knowledge, let alone set out a syllogism ('Nothing is easier to erase than a dialectical effect', he quips in *Twilight of the Idols*, 1889).

Under the influence of the Materialists and also Schopenhauer, Nietzsche took consciousness and reason to play a rather minor role in what humans do, believe and value; far more important are our unconscious and subconscious instinctive and affective lives. In *Beyond Good and Evil* (1886), Nietzsche writes that what inspires 'mistrust and mockery' of the great philosophers is that,

> They all pose as if they had discovered and
> arrived at their genuine convictions through the
> self-development of a cold, pure, divinely
> indifferent dialectic ... while what really happens
> is that they take a conjecture, a whim, an
> 'inspiration' or, more typically, they take some
> fervent wish that they have sifted through and
> made properly abstract – and they defend it with
> rationalisations after the fact. They are all
> advocates who do not want to be seen as such ...

Recall that even Kant finally admitted his goal was to put limits on reason to 'make room for faith' – in God and in morality. But Nietzsche will not partake in this charade of offering post-hoc rationalisations for metaphysical theses that are really motivated by 'the moral (or immoral) intentions' of the philosopher, for it is these intentions which 'constitute the real germ from which the whole plant [i.e. the philosophical system] has always grown'. Nietzsche's motivations are, by his own admission, 'immoral' ones.

Superficial readers who think Nietzsche defends a 'metaphysics of will to power' must ignore his own 'mistrust and mockery' of such philosophical extravagance: achieving a 'feeling of power' is an important human motivation, as he argues in *On the Genealogy of Morality* (1887), but that is a psychological, not metaphysical, claim. For Nietzsche the psychologist, the moral views of a philosopher also 'bear decided and decisive witness to *who he is* – which means, in what order of rank the innermost drives of his nature stand with respect to each other'. But non-rational drives can be influenced and redirected primarily by non-rational means: if you provoke, amuse and annoy the reader, you thereby arouse his affects (drives are, on Nietzsche's view, dispositions to have certain kinds of affective responses). Thus, Nietzsche's mode of writing grows out of his conception of what humans, including philosophers, are really like.

On this view, our conscious selves are largely illusory – 'consciousness *is* a surface', Nietzsche says in *Ecce Homo* (1888), one that conceals the causally efficacious, but unconscious, drives. 'The greatest part of our spirit's activity … remains unconscious and unfelt' (*The Gay Science*, 1882), while 'everything of which we become conscious … causes nothing' (*The Will to Power*, 1901; 1906). When we speak of the 'will' or of the 'motive' that precedes an action, we are speaking merely of 'error[s]' and 'phantoms', 'merely a surface phenomenon of consciousness – something alongside the deed that is more likely to cover up the antecedents of the deed than to represent them' (*Twilight of the Idols*). Humans are, on Nietzsche's view, neither free nor morally responsible for their actions.

But the illusion of free will is not the main reason he rejects Judeo-Christian morality. 'It is *not* error as error' (*Ecce Homo*) that he objects to in such morality. Nietzsche's central objection to morality is more radical and illiberal: any culture dominated by Judeo-Christian morality, or other ascetic or life-denying moralities, will be one inhospitable to the realisation of human excellence. What if, as he says in *On the Genealogy of Morality*, 'morality itself were to blame if the *highest power and splendor* possible to the type man was never in fact attained? So that morality itself was the danger of dangers?'

Consider his objection to moral views that demand we eliminate suffering and promote happiness. In *Dawn* (1881), he writes, 'Are we not, with this tremendous objective of obliterating all the sharp edges of life, well on the way to turning mankind into *sand*? Sand! Small, soft, round, unending sand! Is that your ideal, you heralds of the sympathetic affections?' In *Beyond Good and Evil* a few years later, he objects to utilitarians that, 'Well-being as you understand it – that is no goal, that seems to us an *end*, a state that soon makes man ridiculous and contemptible ...'

Does a focus on happiness really make people 'ridiculous and contemptible'? Nietzsche offers a more ambitious explanation in *Beyond Good and Evil*:

> The discipline of suffering, of *great* suffering – do you not know that only *this* discipline has created all enhancements of man so far? That tension of the soul in unhappiness which cultivates its strength, its shudders face to face with great ruin, its inventiveness and courage in enduring, persevering, interpreting, and exploiting suffering, and whatever has been granted to it of profundity, secret, mask, spirit, cunning, greatness – was it not granted to it through suffering, through the discipline of great suffering?

Most suffering is nothing more than misery for its subject, and most happy 'comfortable' people are not exemplars of human excellence. Nietzsche surely knew this. (He was no 'tourist' when it came to suffering – even before his disability-related retirement from Basel in 1879, and continuing on until his final mental collapse in 1889, he suffered from excruciating physical maladies, probably due to untreated syphilis.) What Nietzsche noticed is that suffering, at least in certain individuals (including himself), could be the stimulus to extraordinary creativity – one need only read a biography of Beethoven to see a paradigmatic example. But even if Nietzsche has correctly diagnosed the psychological mechanism at work, why should a morality of pity for suffering present an obstacle to sufferers realising their creative potential? Nietzsche's crucial thought is that in a culture committed to happiness and the elimination of suffering as its goal, nascent Nietzsches and Beethovens will squander their potential in pursuit of both those aims, rather than in pursuing creative work. After all, if it is *bad* to suffer, then all your efforts should be devoted to avoiding suffering; and if it is *good* to be happy, then that should be the aim of everything you do. *But human excellence is compatible with neither the pursuit of happiness nor the flight from suffering.*

If Nietzsche's speculative psychology is correct, then we arrive at a startling conclusion. In a hedonistic and sympathetic culture, which devalues suffering and prioritises its relief, the glorious spectacle of human genius will be missing from the world: no Beethovens, Nietzsches or Goethes. And absent these creative geniuses Nietzsche thinks we cannot respond to Schopenhauer's existential challenge.

Schopenhauer, recall, deemed life not worth living given the inevitability of pointless suffering. The animating idea of Nietzsche's response to Schopenhauer remained steady from the beginning to the end of his career. As he puts it in the new 1886 preface to *The Birth of Tragedy*: 'the existence of the world is *justified* only as an aesthetic phenomenon', one that 'seduc[es] one to a continuation of life'. Crucially, Nietzsche's account of aesthetic experience is wholly opposed to Kant's idea that the experience of the beautiful is 'disinterested'. Nietzsche endorses Stendhal's formula for aesthetic experience, namely, that 'the beautiful *promises* happiness'; that is, it produces 'the *arousal of the will* ("of interest")', as he puts it in the *Genealogy*. The description of aesthetic experience as involving 'arousal' is not at all accidental: as Nietzsche writes later on in the *Genealogy*, 'the peculiar sweetness and fullness characteristic of the aesthetic condition ... might have its origins precisely in ... "sensuality"' though it is now 'transfigure[d] and no longer enters consciousness as sexual stimulus'.

Aesthetic experience is, in short, *arousing*, a kind of sublimated sexual experience. 'Art is the great stimulus to life' (*Twilight of the Idols*), one that arouses feelings that make its subject want to be alive. But life can only be aesthetically pleasing (arousing) if we continue to enjoy the spectacle of genius, precisely what Nietzsche thinks Judeo-Christian morality threatens. What 'makes life on earth worth living', Nietzsche says in *Beyond Good and Evil* are things like 'virtue, art, music, dance, reason, intellect – something that transfigures, something refined, fantastic, and divine'. But if these kinds of excellences of human achievement are not possible in a culture devoted to hedonistic satisfaction and obsessed with eliminating all forms of suffering (from the trivial to the serious), then we will have no response to Schopenhauer's nihilism.

In *Thus Spoke Zarathustra* (1883–1885) Nietzsche envisioned such a culture, one dominated by those he called 'the last men', who know nothing of 'love' or 'creation' or 'longing', who are unable to 'despise' themselves because of their 'wretched contentment', while wallowing in their own mediocrity. The last man 'knows everything that has ever happened: so there is no end of derision'. 'Everybody wants the same, everybody is the same: whoever feels different goes voluntarily into a madhouse.' 'We have invented happiness', say the last men, 'and they blink.'

Brian Leiter directs the Center for Law, Philosophy & Human Values at the University of Chicago. He is the author of Nietzsche on Morality, 2nd ed., 2015, and Moral Psychology with Nietzsche, 2019.

Simone Weil

by A. Rebecca Rozelle-Stone

It is safe to assume that Simone Weil (1909–1943), the French philosopher and social activist, would not have approved of the state of the modern world. Excessive consumption is glamorised, environmental limits are blithely ignored, sadism has become a media spectacle, and the truth holds little value in our age of distraction. Weil would see no mere coincidence in the idea that as the facts of our world become ever bleaker, our technology and popular culture increasingly encourage a flight from the demands of reality.

She understood from her own context that the desire to turn a blind eye to the world – itself originating in deep dissatisfaction with the present state of things – ends up exacerbating the moral disaster. Fascism was on the rise in Europe throughout much of Weil's short life, as were the related evils of a capitalist expansionism already threatening the Earth's resources, and the growing mechanisation of (and alienation produced by) various forms of labour. Suffering may encourage escapist tendencies, but she saw first-hand the ways in which escapism only creates more societal imbalance and therefore suffering. As she reflected in her *Notebooks*, 'Modern life is *given over to excess*. Everything is steeped in it – thought as well as action, private life as well as public ... There is no more equilibrium anywhere'.

From an early age, Weil had a desire to know, on an unfiltered level, people from all backgrounds and stations of life, and particularly those who were marginalised. At the age of five, Simone and her brother André (later a famous mathematician) 'adopted' a French soldier fighting in the First World War, and Weil used her pocket money to create care packages which she sent to her soldier. When she was ten, Weil and a group of her friends created a club they called 'the Knights of the Round Table', as part of which they swore to defend the innocent, and to practise charity. At eleven, Weil joined workers who were on strike on the Boulevard Saint Michel, just below her family's apartment.

As an adult, when she began teaching philosophy at a girls' school in Le Puy, Weil gave away most of her salary to welfare funds, assistance agencies and the solidarity fund for the miners of Saint-Étienne. In 1934 she took a year's leave from her comfortable teaching job to work in various factories in Paris that she might better understand the workers' plight – an experience that put her in touch with the ugly reality of Taylorist work on the conveyor belts. Later, a trip to Germany as the Nazi movement took hold persuaded Weil to renounce her pacifism, and she joined the Spanish Civil War in 1936 to support the Loyalists (although she didn't last long, burning herself badly after stepping into a pot of cooking oil). Even the manner of her death attested to her solidarity with the suffering. Though living in England and working as part of the French Resistance, Weil would not allow herself to eat more than she believed her fellow citizens were permitted under German occupation. She was already in poor health and suffering from tuberculosis, and died on August 24, 1943, at Grosvenor Sanitorium in Kent.

But Weil herself was no stranger to the temptations of mental escape. She wrote extensively in her notebooks, letters and essays about the pull towards base pleasures, feel-good narratives, nostalgia, mass delusion and fantasies that provide a false sense of comfort. In a letter of 1941 to Father Perrin, a nearly blind Dominican priest in whom she confided and corresponded with, Weil described the dangers of collective enthusiasms, even admitting, incredibly, that if she were standing before 'a group of twenty young Germans singing Nazi songs in chorus', a part of her soul 'would instantly become Nazi'. This sort of confession was typical: Weil was exacting in her self-appraisals. And she nursed a strong desire for group belonging which she understood to be highly problematic. Her vocation, she believed, was to serve the truth, and this meant abstaining from joining collectives – whether the Catholic Church or any organisation or political party – so that she could 'move among people of every class and complexion, mixing with them and sharing their life and outlook … merging into the crowd and disappearing among them'.

Weil's ideas culminated in what we might call an 'ethics of attention', where attention is understood to mean receptivity to and rootedness in reality with a vigilant and patient disposition – an idea she articulated in her famous essay, 'Reflections on the Right Use of School Studies with a View to the Love of God', written for Father Perrin in 1942. Practically speaking, attention is also a call to resist flight from our own discomfort when it results from the awareness of pain or misfortune. To resist escapism and endure the discomfort ushered in by recognising reality is to experience 'the void', to use Weil's terminology. The void, for her, is a religious concept, and it recurs throughout her later notebooks (1941–1942). It is a core part of our being as humans – a remnant of God's refusal to be everything through the act of creating something outside of Himself. For Weil, the fact of being created via divine self-abdication means that an experiential vacuum, a permanent and original wound, is the marker of every self-conscious being. In a non-religious sense, to sit with the void is to experience an ultimate silence, an abyss of meaning, a felt absence, the pain of a loss, the humiliation of being wrong, a sense of incompletion and finitude, or simply the vulnerability that accompanies being mortal. In short, the void announces itself as a feeling of psychic and physical disequilibrium underpinned by a longing for completion (which is absent). But this is only a reflection of the true state of things. 'We must prefer real hell to an imaginary paradise', Weil admonishes us in her *Notebooks*.

Yet the void irritates like an itch, and it produces restlessness, for either boredom or existential anxiety usually awaits us in our encounter with it. Thus, we seek to restore balance and ease by 'filling the void'. As soon as we feel the discomfort announced by the void, compensatory and consoling thoughts, ideas, images, and distractions rush in to re-establish a sense of equilibrium. Such compensations derive from the self-preserving ego and its imaginings, and, like bad fiction born of the impatience to publish, the resulting dreams are flat, two-dimensional and simplistic. These fantasies, Weil tells us, have destroyed the third dimension, for only real objects have three dimensions, multiple relationships, texture, and nuance. As she reflected in her *Notebooks*: 'A test of what is real is that it is hard and rough. Joys are found in it, not pleasure. Everything that is pleasurable is merely reverie'. The proper disposition to the void we experience (especially during times of loss or suffering) is to acknowledge and endure it, not to disguise, annihilate or try to escape it. To sit with the void, to be calm in the face of the noisy chorus and to maintain our sensitivity throughout the endurance of a crushing reality: this is goodness in action.

On the other hand, for Weil, evil consists in attempting to fill the void by whatever distraction will allow us to feel godlike, invulnerable and limitless. We can understand evil as what results from our restlessness or boredom. Our typical and spectacularised response to boredom and the void that hides behind it is to create chaos, drama, clamour and provocation. There is even social-scientific evidence for this connection: in a recent study, published in the *Journal of Personality and Social Psychology* in 2021, psychologists suggest that boredom plays a crucial role in the emergence of sadistic tendencies. Blaise Pascal wrote in his *Pensées* that we detest nothing more than a lack of diversion in which we are left to reflect on our mortal human condition. In this sense, distracting our leaders with amusements so that they do not have time to think is pragmatic:

> Let us leave a king all alone to reflect on himself
> quite at leisure, without any gratification of the
> senses, without any care in his mind, without

society; and we will see that a king without
diversion is a man full of wretchedness. So this is
carefully avoided, and near the persons of kings
there never fail to be a great number of people
who see to it that amusement follows business,
and who watch all the time of their leisure to
supply [the kings] with delights and games, so
that there is no blank in it.

The detestation of the void is rooted in the ego and its
desire for activity, in our desire to appropriate the world
for ourselves and forget our inadequacies.

It is no wonder, then, that Weil argues that people are
prone to treat real goodness as unremarkable and boring
while evil is presented as exciting and interesting. Our
entertainment industries reflect these values. Yet the
reality, for Weil, is the opposite. In her article, 'Morality
and Literature', which was published under the anagram-
matic pseudonym Emile Novis in the journal *Cahiers du
Sud* a year after her death, Weil begins:

Nothing is so beautiful and wonderful, nothing is
so continually fresh and surprising, so full of
sweet and perpetual ecstasy, as the good. No
desert is so dreary, monotonous, and boring as
evil. This is the truth about authentic good and
evil. With fictional good and evil it is the other

way round. Fictional good is boring and flat,
while fictional evil is varied and intriguing,
attractive, profound, and full of charm.

She goes on to say that there are 'necessities and impossibilities in reality' which need not be present in fiction. As a result, the sense of limitlessness with which our imaginations play can produce wild scenarios and characters that are not beholden to natural laws, consequences or material conditions. The psychopaths and monsters that fill our screens and pages today, from Hannibal Lecter to Logan Roy, are presented as psychologically complex, conflicted and sometimes sympathetic. Audiences are simultaneously shocked and enthralled by the audacity of these characters' crimes and their lack of conscience. Evil here is the ultimate freedom.

Yet Weil reminds us that *real* evil, unlike its scripted counterpart, is stupid and predictable. We find it in the personal insults hurled by politicians who cannot engage in substantive debate. We encounter it in the instigators and executors of mass violence who cannot stand the fact of their own vulnerability. We see the banality of evil in every type of prejudice and small-minded hatred – the simplicity of thought that condemns entire groups of people based on arbitrary qualities derived from tribalistic tendencies, irrational fears and insecure egos.

Conversely, one who is capable of enduring the void, of renouncing flights from reality and of giving genuine loving attention to a fellow being, is, in Weil's thinking, the embodiment of a miracle. To be attentive to one who is afflicted, even by sincerely asking the simple question 'What are you going through?', is rare and difficult. In part this is because many of those who suffer have been made invisible to us: they have been ghettoised, contained in detention centres, shelters and prisons, increasingly restricted from public places except for encampments on the perimeters of cities and under highway overpasses and refugee camps. Often destitute and socially unrecognised, they have been deprived of their voices, and in any case may 'have no words to express what is happening to them', as Weil puts it in her essay, 'The Love of God and Affliction' (1942). So compassion is practically all but impossible, according to Weil. 'When it is really found', she writes, 'we have a more astounding miracle than walking on water, healing the sick, or even raising the dead.'

Perhaps this is why it is so unusual – unthinkable almost – to see a representation of true goodness on our screens and in our cultural milieux. A real saint would be practically anonymous, simply a vehicle for supernatural love to touch those who have been exiled, disregarded and downtrodden. Goodness would consist in a genuine encounter, with all of the vulnerability and honesty that entails. To be good requires courage to deal justly and openly with the raw material that reality provides, while refraining from fictionalising the world or projecting onto others. Nor can the act of attention be a spectacle for other people, for that would exploit the recipient of the gesture and turn the act of giving into a performance of pseudo-generosity. A person inspired by Weil to live a morally attentive existence may never receive recognition, but then they would not seek it, either. The joy and edification, and the beautiful surprises that come from meaningful gestures of solidarity and love, would be sufficient.

A. Rebecca Rozelle-Stone is Chester Fritz Distinguished Professor of Philosophy and Ethics at the University of North Dakota. She is the author of Simone Weil: A Very Short Introduction, *2024, and editor of* Simone Weil and Continental Philosophy, *2017.*

Acknowledgements

I'd like to thank all the contributors to *Footnotes to Plato* who produced a wonderful collection of essays over the years – both those whose work appears in this book, and all the others who contributed to our online series. Stig Abell was instrumental in supporting the original series, and Martin Ivens strongly encouraged the production of this book. I'd like to thank David Roth-Ey, Myles Archibald and Eva Hodgkin at HarperCollins. And from the *TLS*, Lucy Dallas, Robert Potts, Will Eaves and George Berridge.

Also from TLS Books

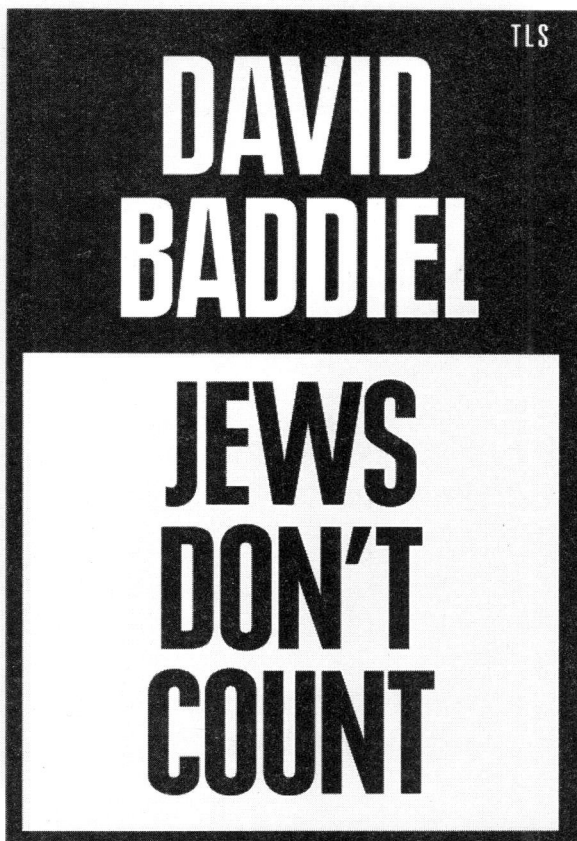

How identity politics failed one particular identity.

'The whole book is just brilliant -
and very much needed'
Simon Schama

Also from TLS Books

The bestselling author of the Jack Reacher
books explores what makes a hero

Also from TLS Books

Join the art critic Ben Eastham on a
private tour of an extraordinary museum.

Also from TLS Books

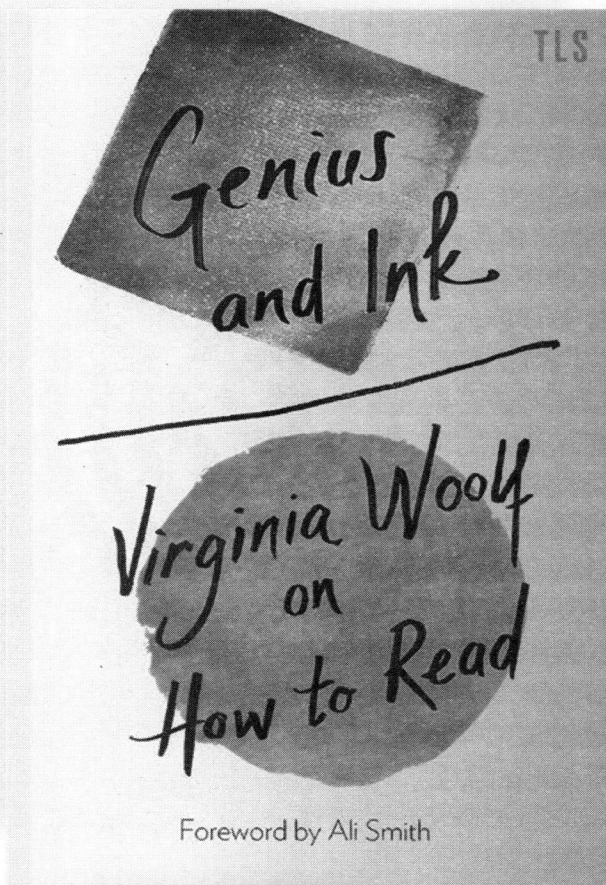

Who better to serve as a guide to great books and their authors than Virginia Woolf?

Also from TLS Books

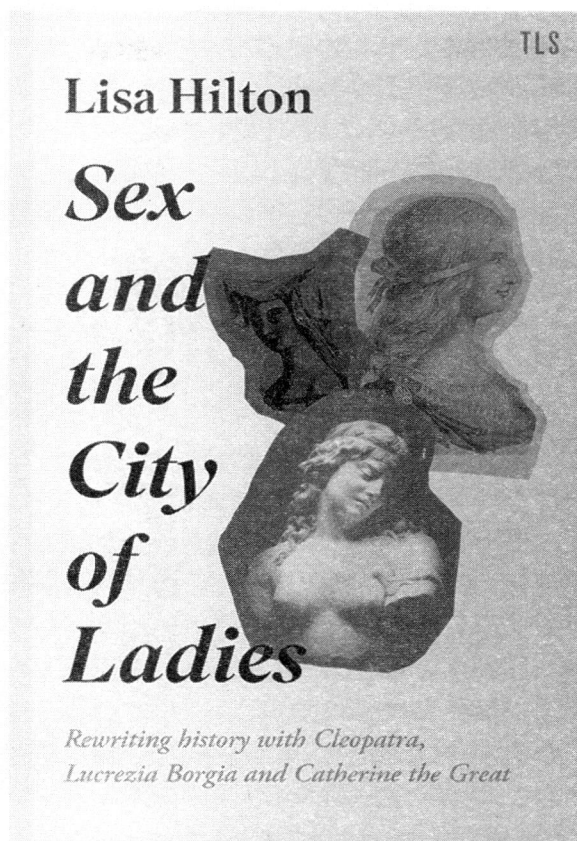

Lisa Hilton picks up the mythical 'City of Ladies'
where the medieval writer Christine de Pisan
left off, continuing a conversation about gender
and greatness that began more than six hundred
years ago.

Also from TLS Books

PATRICIA WILLIAMS

GIVING A DAMN

RACISM, ROMANCE AND
GONE WITH THE WIND

TLS

How was the USA, the richest and most diverse
nation on the planet, brought to the brink of
resurgent violent division?

The answer begins with slavery.